CLIP CULTURE
MANUAL 2

CLIP CULTURE MANUAL 2

The Cheat Code

DAVID MICHAEL BROWN

MYND MATTERS

Books may be purchased in bulk quantity and/or special sales by contacting the publisher.

Mynd Matters Publishing
2690 Cobb Parkway SE
Ste A5-375
Smyrna, GA 30080
www.myndmatterspublishing.com

978-1-963874-02-0 (pbk)
978-1-963874-03-7 (hdcv)
978-1-963874-04-4 (ebk)

FIRST EDITION

CONTENTS

MAMA, YOU THE INSPIRATION.

INTRODUCTION

C*lip Culture Manual 2: The Cheat Code* serves as a game-changing source tailored for entrepreneurs seeking a strategic advantage in business. Drawing from a diverse array of real-world scenarios and urban wisdom, *Clip Culture Manual 2* is more than just a guide—it's a cheat code for success.

From navigating the intricacies of permits to mastering the art of storytelling and essential tools for grown men, each chapter unlocks valuable insights and tactics. Written in a conversational and relatable tone, this manual empowers entrepreneurs to overcome challenges, make informed decisions, and elevate their business game.

With a blend of street-smart advice and practical strategies, it's a must-have companion for those ready to level up their entrepreneurial journey.

CURATING SUCCESS: THE STRATEGIC ART OF PRESELECTION IN BUSINESS AND RELATIONSHIPS

Entering new business or personal relationships is akin to assembling a tribe. The cornerstone of this process? Preselection—a strategic method of candidate selection often driven by referrals. It's not just a practice, it's a fundamental necessity for navigating the complex terrain of connections.

When venturing into uncharted territories, whether in business or forging personal friendships, blindly accepting everything that comes your way is a risky endeavor. Adequate screening, akin to the concept of preselection, becomes your shield against potential time drains, emotional pains, and unnecessary expenses.

Preselection serves as a mirror reflecting the composition of your current circle. It doesn't guarantee approval. Rather, it signifies alignment with certain criteria established by the organization or, in personal relationships, by your values and aspirations. It's not about being accepted by everyone but about filtering through to find those whose vibes resonate with your own.

In this intricate dance of connections, preselection offers a 70% chance of approval—a favorable ratio that hints at the potential harmony and synergy awaiting you. So, as you curate your tribe, remember the power of preselection. It's not just about who you let in. It's about building a community that aligns with your vision and values.

In the symphony of connections, preselection emerges as your orchestrator—a discerning guide in the pursuit of meaningful relationships. Assemble your tribe wisely, embracing the art of preselection, and watch how the harmony of shared values and visions elevates your personal and professional journey.

PROACTIVE VIBES: COMBATTING THE INACTION IN YOUR BUSINESS

In the bustling world of business, the term "the inaction" takes center stage—an ominous phenomenon characterized by the absence of expected or appropriate action. For entrepreneurs, this is a call to arms. A reminder that the success of your establishment hinges not only on what you do but also on what your team does.

Picture this: individuals in your establishment who witness tasks that need attention but choose inaction. It's not just a lack of movement, it's a silent statement that reverberates through the core of your business. As a business owner, your brand is a living entity, and every member of your team is a custodian of its essence.

The inaction, often underestimated, holds the potential to be as detrimental, if not more, than blatant negative actions. Customers, the lifeblood of your business, are concerned solely with their experience and the service they receive. To deliver the best, you must cultivate a culture of proactive engagement within your team.

So, if you spot inaction taking root in your business, it's time for action. It's a reflection on your brand, and you owe it to yourself and your customers to foster an environment where every individual takes pride in actively contributing to the success of your establishment.

Real talk, the silent stagnation of inaction within your business can speak louder than any proactive efforts. As a business owner, it's crucial to foster an environment where action is not just encouraged but expected. Your brand's reputation hinges on the collective effort of your team. Prioritize not only what is done but also what isn't. Customers deserve an experience that reflects the vitality of a business in constant motion.

YOUR **BRAND** IS A LIVING **ENTITY,** AND **EVERY** MEMBER OF YOUR **TEAM** IS A CUSTODIAN OF ITS **ESSENCE.**

STREET SMARTS: THE ART OF EFFECTIVE OUTSIDE SIGNAGE

I n the world of business, envision your storefront as a canvas, and the outdoor signage as the brushstroke defining your presence in the urban landscape. When establishing your physical footprint, grabbing attention is the primary objective, transcending mere signage to create a lasting imprint in the minds of those who pass by.

Within the swift current of traffic, you're granted a mere three seconds to etch your business into the minds of potential clients. Consider your signage as a beacon, succinctly encapsulating the essence of your enterprise at a single glance—an impactful visual introduction, even if they don't step inside immediately.

Building brand recognition is a gradual journey, and the initial signage serves as a crucial seed of curiosity. While aspirations may involve iconic logos gracing your storefront, simplicity is the initial strategy. Prioritize clarity to effectively communicate your business offerings. As your brand evolves into a symbol of excellence, your logo will organically transform into a beacon, instantly recognizable to those in the know.

The mastery of outside signage extends beyond

mere visibility. It's about leaving an indelible mark on the urban canvas. Approach this strategically, recognizing that each detail contributes to the overarching narrative of your business in the cityscape. In essence, your strategic investment in outside signage goes beyond catching attention. It crafts a lasting impression that resonates with potential clients, seamlessly integrating into the community landscape.

MAINTAIN THE AESTHETICS

When you're in the hustle of running a business, the need for touch-up paint is inevitable. It's like a rite of passage. Scuffs happen, accidents occur, and your space may need a little sprucing up. Having a trusty gallon of paint on standby is a smart move. Consider it your secret weapon against the wear and tear of daily operations.

Just like a home, your business demands constant upkeep. It's a cycle of wear, tear, and repair. Remember, your space is a reflection of your brand. Those scuffs on the walls, side panels, or trim might seem minor, but they can subtly affect the perception of your business.

If you didn't save the original paint gallons, don't fret. Snap a picture of the label and save it as a favorite—consider it your virtual backup. This simple practice can be a lifesaver when you need to match the color precisely.

Approaching the task is an art. Before applying that touch-up paint, wipe down the areas with a dry cloth for a clean canvas. Consider keeping a sander handy for more significant touch-ups. It's these small details that will keep your business looking sharp and professional.

In essence, touch-up paint isn't merely a practical solution for scuffs and marks, it's a commitment to presenting your business in the best light. As you take the time for these small but impactful touches, you're investing in the overall impression your space makes. So, grab that gallon, touch up those scuffs, and watch how these seemingly minor details contribute to the vibrancy and professionalism that define your brand. Your business deserves to shine, one brushstroke at a time.

PAPER TRAIL WISDOM: GUARDING YOUR BUSINESS

I n the ever-evolving dance of life and business, one universal truth prevails— protect yourself at all costs. When it comes to the realm of entrepreneurship, the need for next-level coverage becomes non-negotiable. Enter C.Y.A—Cover Yo Ass—an essential mantra to  navigate the intricate web of transactions and dealings.

Consider documentation a shield, your armor against potential pitfalls. Keep a meticulous paper trail of transactions, bills, and payments. In the absence of receipts, vulnerabilities emerge, and the unscrupulous may seek to exploit any gaps. Not everyone you encounter has your best interests at heart, and the absence of a clear record can be a costly oversight.

The power of ink on paper should never be underestimated. Having agreements notarized elevates them from mere words to binding commitments. Once pen meets paper and the ink dries, a deal is more than a handshake, it's a contractual and legal obligation. No matter the subsequent maneuvers, the contract stands as a testament to the agreed-upon terms, a fortress that demands adherence.

So, fellow entrepreneurs, safeguard your journey with a commitment to record-keeping. Every receipt, email, and contract is a building block, fortifying your business against uncertainties. These seemingly mundane documents are your insurance policy, ready to step in when needed most.

Embracing the ethos of C.Y.A is not just about paperwork. It's a strategic move to secure your business's legacy. As you amass a trail of evidence, you're not merely covering yourself, you're fortifying the foundations of your entrepreneurial empire—one signature, one receipt, one notarized agreement at a time. Because in the business realm, vigilant documentation is the true mark of a savvy entrepreneur.

CRAFTSMANSHIP CHRONICLES: UNLEASHING THE POWER OF FREE WORK

In the grand tapestry of entrepreneurship, there exists a pivotal chapter—the art of offering your craft without a price tag. "The Free Work is the Key Work" is more than a principle, it's a philosophy that transcends monetary transactions, forging connections rooted in genuine appreciation for the craft.

In the hustle and grind of business, there comes a time when giving work away becomes a strategic move. It's not about diminishing your worth. Rather, it's a profound expression of your passion for the art. Beyond the allure of financial gains, there lies a deeper narrative—the story of authenticity, passion, and the art of storytelling.

True craftsmanship extends beyond being the best. It's about weaving a narrative that resonates with authenticity. Clients can discern genuine enthusiasm, recognizing the synergy between passion and skill. This alignment creates a powerful force that captivates, leaving an indelible mark on the canvas of your business.

When you offer your craft freely, you embark on a journey of appreciation—for your skill, the grind, and the individuals who champion your business. It's a subtle nod to the essence of longevity. Every act of generosity becomes a beacon, attracting unforeseen opportunities and opening doors to uncharted territories.

However, it's crucial to strike a balance. Passion and skill should harmonize with pricing and enthusiasm. A misalignment sticks out like a sore thumb, hindering the organic growth of your business. The key lies in a symbiotic relationship—appreciation for  the craft, dedication to the grind, and gratitude for the unwavering support of your clientele.

In a nutshell, "Free Work is the Key Work" is not a concession. It's a strategic move that propels your narrative forward. As you navigate the complexity of business, remember that sometimes, the most profound stories emerge when you let the craft speak for itself, unburdened by price tags. It's a journey that transforms transactions into tales, weaving a legacy that withstands the tests of time.

ELEVATING YOUR VISUAL GAME: UNLEASHING CREATIVITY WITH VIDEO EDITING

When it comes to content creation, having the right tools at your disposal can make all the difference. One such tool that has proven its worth for me is the VideoLeap app. This handy video editing app opens up a world of creative possibilities for entrepreneurs looking to elevate their content game.

Unlocking Creativity:
In the dynamic realm of digital content, innovation is key. VideoLeap provides a platform for turning your ideas into engaging visual stories. From captivating time lapses to celebrity-inspired cuts and intricate designs, the app empowers you to bring your creative visions to life.

Time lapses that Tell Stories:
Time-lapse videos are a unique way to capture and share the passage of time. Whether it's showcasing the evolution of your business space or highlighting a behind-the-scenes process, time lapses add a dynamic element to your content that keeps viewers hooked.

Celebrity Cuts:
Ever admired the editing style of your favorite celebrities? Now, you can infuse that same star-quality flair into your own content. VideoLeap offers tools to create sleek and professional cuts, ensuring your videos stand out in the crowded digital landscape.

Designs that Dazzle:
Visual appeal is everything in the world of online content. With VideoLeap, you can effortlessly incorporate stunning designs into your videos. Elevate your brand aesthetics and leave a lasting impression on your audience with eye-catching visuals that speak volumes.

In the competitive arena of digital storytelling, VideoLeap emerges as a valuable ally. Experiment with time lapses, channel your inner celebrity editor, and craft designs that dazzle. With VideoLeap, your content becomes a canvas for unlimited creativity, allowing you to set your brand apart in the online landscape.

Crafting Captivating Visuals:
Pro Tips for Seamless Video Editing

In the fast-paced world of digital content, the way you present your message matters. To help you navigate the landscape of video editing, here are some practical tips and tricks that can make a significant difference:

Setting the Right Tone with Music:
When it comes to creating engaging videos, the soundtrack sets the tone. Utilize trending or popular songs as background music to enhance the overall impact of your content. A well-chosen track can elevate the mood and captivate your audience from the first second.

The Power of Voiceovers:
Sometimes, words are as essential as visuals. Consider adding voiceovers to provide context, narration, or to convey a message directly. Voiceovers add a personal touch, helping you connect with your audience on a deeper level.

Precision Cutting for Impact:
Effective storytelling often involves concise and impactful editing. Use your editing app to cut videos with precision. Trimming unnecessary footage ensures that your message remains focused, holding the viewer's attention throughout.

Embrace Brevity:
In the attention-deficit digital age, brevity is king. Keep your videos concise, aiming for a duration of no longer than forty-five seconds. This not only caters to shorter attention spans but also encourages viewers to absorb your message quickly and effortlessly.

Enhancing Accessibility with Subtitles:

To broaden the accessibility of your content, consider adding subtitles. Subtitles not only cater to a diverse audience but also ensure that your message is understood, even in sound-sensitive environments.

Closing the Edit:

In the ever-evolving landscape of content creation, mastering these editing tips and tricks can set you apart. Whether it's the impactful use of music, the personal touch of voiceovers, or the art of precision cutting, each element contributes to crafting compelling narratives that resonate.

As you embark on your journey of crafting

compelling content through video editing, remember that every cut, every sound, and every second plays a role in shaping the narrative. By embracing these tips and tricks, you're not just editing videos, you're creating an experience. The power of storytelling lies in your hands, and with the right tools, your content can captivate, resonate, and leave a lasting impact. So, go ahead, hit that export button, and share your story with the world. Let your creativity flow and your message unfold, making every video a testament to your unique voice in the digital realm.

VISUAL BRILLIANCE UNLEASHED: EXPERT TECHNIQUES TO ELEVATE YOUR VIDEOGRAPHY

E levating your videography skills to an unparalleled level demands a seamless blend of professionalism and urban sophistication. Tailored for the discerning creator navigating the intersection of ultra-professionalism and the dynamic urban landscape, here's a curated fusion of refined tips.

1. Illuminate with Precision: Elevate Your Lighting Precision

In the concrete jungle, where every detail matters, a

ring light becomes your beacon of precision. Invest in a high-quality ring light to sculpt the perfect illumination for your videos. This ensures not only consistent and flattering lighting but also sets the stage for a visually stunning narrative.

2. Cinematic Brilliance: Craft Your Visual Symphony

In the urban landscape, where visual storytelling is an art form, leverage the Cinematic Mode of your camera app. This feature transcends utility, it's your gateway to cinematic brilliance. Explore its capabilities to introduce a shallow depth of field, adding a touch of sophistication befitting the professionalism your brand demands.

3. Comprehensive Storytelling: Unveil the Full Narrative Spectrum

In the intricate tapestry of urban services, precision storytelling is paramount. Film the entirety of your services—start, middle, and ending. This approach transforms your videos into immersive narratives, providing a holistic view that resonates with your audience's discerning taste for detail.

4. Before and After Mastery: Dynamic Transitions for Captivating Stories

In the urban hustle, dynamic storytelling is your

signature move. Master the "before and after" camera work to unveil transformations with flair. Guide the camera to a concealed space, commence recording, seamlessly transition to a new recording in the same enigmatic place, and skillfully pan out. This technique adds an element of anticipation and visual allure to your content.

As you weave these refined techniques into your videography repertoire, remember that every frame is an opportunity to showcase urban elegance. Tailor these tips to align with the distinctive character of your brand, creating visual narratives that seamlessly blend professionalism with an urban edge.

Elevating Technique:
A Cinematic Symphony in Videography
Taking your videography skills to the zenith requires a keen eye for detail and a touch of cinematic finesse. Explore these expert tips that not only enhance the technical aspects of your content but also infuse creativity for an unforgettable visual storytelling experience.

5. Illuminate with a Ring Light: Elevate Your Lighting Precision
Invest in a quality ring light to attain professional lighting mastery. Whether capturing diverse environments or intricate details up close, a ring light ensures consistent

and flattering illumination. This subtle addition significantly enhances the overall visual appeal of your content.

6. Cinematic Brilliance with Camera App's Cinematic Mode: Craft Your Visual Symphony

Delve into your camera app's Cinematic Mode to add a touch of cinematic magic. This feature creates a shallow depth of field reminiscent of professional films. Experiment with Cinematic Mode to infuse your content with a polished and visually stunning quality that captivates your audience.

7. Comprehensive Storytelling: Unveil the Full Narrative Spectrum

Capture the entire narrative spectrum by filming the start, middle, and ending of any services or scenarios. This comprehensive approach weaves a seamless and engaging visual story, providing viewers with a holistic understanding and a more immersive experience.

8. Before and After Magic: Dynamic Transitions for Captivating Stories

Learn the art of before and after camera work to introduce a dynamic element to your content. Guide the camera to a dark area, commence recording, seamlessly transition to a new recording in the same enigmatic place, and gradually pan out. This technique builds anticipation and highlights the evolution of your subject matter.

Experiment with these videography tips, ensuring they align with your brand's unique style and messaging. Craft visually compelling stories that not only enhance the technical aspects of your content but also resonate creatively, leaving an indelible impression on your audience.

CRAFTING YOUR ENTREPRENEURIAL TALE: A GUIDE TO ENGAGING CONTENT CREATION

Mastering the art of content creation is like conducting a symphony of visuals, capturing the essence of your entrepreneurial journey. Picture this: a daily dose of your hustle in thirty-day posts, a weekly cinematic exploration of your four-hour workday, and sprinkling in fifteen golden nuggets, each lasting fifteen to thirty seconds. But here's the real secret sauce. Diversity is the spice that keeps your audience hooked.

Take them on a journey through the corridors of your daily life, unraveling the unique aspects of your entrepreneurial routine. The captions, though short, are the storytellers that breathe life into each frame. Craft them to provide context, pose questions, and ignite interaction.

Now, let's talk aesthetics. A consistent color grade is your signature, the visual thread weaving through your brand's aesthetic tapestry. Choose a color palette that resonates with your brand's essence, making each piece of content instantly recognizable.

But amidst all these, there's one cardinal rule—keep your viewers' attention at the forefront. It's not just about content. It's about creating an experience that captivates and resonates.

So, as you embark on this content creation journey, remember that every post, film, and nugget is a brushstroke on the canvas of your brand's narrative. Let each one reflect your passion, creativity, and commitment to leaving an indelible mark in the digital realm.

YOU CAN

NEVER SELL

YOUR WAY OUT

OF A BAD

DEAL.

BUSINESS WISDOM: NAVIGATING THE GAME WITH REAL TALK

Alright, let's cut to the chase. In business, you need more than just dreams. You need a solid game plan. Here's some real talk for you:

Have a Formula, Stay Unemotional: Money Talks

Listen up, it's business, not a soap opera. Develop a formula and stick to it like glue. Emotions can cloud your judgment. The real cash comes from smart purchases. Buying right is your ticket to success. Remember, you can't sell your way out of a bad deal.

Master Your Formula: Franchise Your Success

You've been around the block, right? Once you've nailed your formula, it's time to level up. Ever thought about franchising your business model? It's the next step for a seasoned player like you. Spread your success like wildfire.

Location, Location, Location: It's Everything

You know what they say—location is key. Don't just set up shop anywhere. Connect with an area that's on the upswing, with room to grow. A good school system? Bingo. New developments popping up? Even better. New stores in the neighborhood? Now we're talking. Look for these signs, they're your golden ticket.

Here's the Deal: Be in the Right Place, Right Time
Let's cut through the noise. If you buy or establish your business in a buzzing, upcoming area, you're setting yourself up for a smooth ride. Easier to sell, easier to thrive. Remember this nugget: the main idea is to be in the right place at the right time. So, get your eyes on those signs, and make your move. Navigate the game with wisdom, my friend. #StrategicHustle #BusinessInsights

FINANCIAL INGENUITY: CRAFTING ASSETS TO OFFSET LIABILITIES

Embarking on the entrepreneurial journey feels akin to stepping into a dynamic game of endless possibilities. However, before succumbing to the allure of luxury— envisioning lavish cars, jewelry, watches, and exotic getaways—let's explore a strategic approach that ensures your financial groundwork matches the grandeur of your ambitions.

In this financial narrative, the central principle is clear. Before delving into extravagant purchases, establish assets that seamlessly counteract your liabilities. Picture a scenario where your possessions not only represent indulgences but also serve as robust assets, effortlessly covering your financial responsibilities. Envision a scenario where your investments actively work in your favor, alleviating the need for exhaustive endeavors to fund your desires.

Postpone the allure of flashy expenditures and focus on prioritizing strategic investments. As an entrepreneur, your responsibility lies in creating multiple streams of income that don't merely sustain but flourish. Before entering the realm of opulence, consider investments such as duplexes, stocks, rental properties, and explore unconventional avenues like business partnerships or ventures in the service industry.

Delay the immediate indulgences and concentrate on building wealth first. Understand that genuine success lies not in instant gratification but in enduring triumphs. Duplexes, stocks, and rental properties aren't mere assets, they form the solid foundation of your financial fortress.

Here's the key insight: your primary and secondary business ventures should function as lucrative money-making entities. This isn't just an aspiration, it's a pragmatic reality. When the time arrives to reap the rewards of your endeavors, a harmonious flow of revenue from every entrepreneurial pursuit is the goal.

As an entrepreneur, your role extends beyond the

allure of material desires. It's about making informed decisions, strategically investing, and creating diverse income streams. When the moment arises to revel in your success, it won't be a financial burden. It'll be a well-deserved celebration.

BLESSINGS IN ACTION: THE POWER OF WEEKLY GOOD DEEDS

In the tapestry of life, weaving acts of kindness is not just a gesture, it's a testament to a higher principle. Embracing the biblical wisdom that giving is a pathway to receiving, let's delve into the transformative practice of doing one good deed each week.

This isn't a mere altruistic endeavor, it's a divine exchange. The scripture reminds us of the universal law that as we give, so shall we receive. "Give, and it will be given to you. A good measure, pressed down, shaken together, and running over, will be poured into your lap. For with the measure you use, it will be measured to you" (Luke 6:38, NIV). This principle echoes the essence that selfless acts set in motion a divine reciprocity, and the blessings bestowed upon others ripple back to enrich our lives.

The concept is simple yet profound. Dedicate each week to a good deed. Whether it's a random act of kindness, a thoughtful gift, or uplifting words, these gestures not only impact others positively but also invite divine favor into our own lives. In a year encompassing fifty-two weeks, committing to fifty-two acts of kindness allows us to accumulate a treasury of goodwill.

Staying blessed is not about perfection but growth. As the weeks unfold, you become not only a benefactor to others but also a recipient of unexpected blessings. The goal is to be a better version of yourself than the year before, and this journey of self-improvement is intricately tied to the uplifting of those around you.

The beauty lies in the simplicity—a kind word, a thoughtful gesture, or a surprise gift costs nothing but has the potential to brighten someone's day. By consistently engaging in these acts, you create a positive ripple effect that extends beyond what meets the eye.

Engaging in one good deed each week is more than a routine—it's a tapestry woven with threads of kindness, an investment in the well-being of others, and an open invitation to the divine. As you extend generosity, you unleash a cascade of blessings, enriching not only your own journey but also leaving an indelible mark on the lives touched by your acts of kindness.

DON'T KILL MY VIBE: REMOVING THE VIBE KILLERS

I n the dynamic realm of entrepreneurship, steering clear of vibe killers becomes a vital art. Picture your business as an energetic space where the atmosphere can either fuel growth or hinder progress. Vibe killers, like a cancer, have a knack for spreading negativity that can jeopardize the very essence of your enterprise.

Identifying these energy-draining individuals is crucial, for their influence is contagious. Vibe killers are seldom content. Their dissatisfaction with everything seeps into the fabric of your business. Their negativity clouds the clarity you need to make sound decisions as a business owner.

These individuals, often discontent with their own paths, project their frustrations onto your achievements. Their envy stems from a lack of personal accomplishments, making them resent your strides. Recognizing a vibe killer is the first step, and the best response is simple…ignore.

In essence, your business environment should be a haven of positivity and growth. Eliminating vibe killers ensures that the energy within your entrepreneurial space remains vibrant, fostering an atmosphere conducive to success. Surround yourself with those who uplift, support, and inspire, for in the journey of entrepreneurship, a positive vibe can make all the difference.

MASTERING MONDAYS: A BLUEPRINT FOR A PRODUCTIVE WEEK

In the hustle and bustle of entrepreneurial life, the secret to a successful week lies in the art of intentional preparation. Let's delve into a ritual that can transform your Mondays from chaotic to purposeful, setting the stage for a week of accomplishments.

Navigating the Week Ahead: A Sunday Ritual
Imagine every Sunday evening as a sacred moment where you, as the architect of your destiny, sit down and craft a blueprint for the week. This ritual involves creating a comprehensive list, a roadmap of business calls, personal calls, and essential errands awaiting your attention.

With pen in hand, document these vital tasks, creating a tangible checklist that will be your guide throughout the week. The objective is clear, to step into Monday with a fresh perspective, armed with a clear vision of the objectives that demand your focus.

The Power of a Checklist: Your Weekly Compass

Come Monday morning, armed with your checklist, you embark on a journey of intentionality. Each tick off the list becomes a victory, a step closer to your goals. This process not only organizes your week but also ensures that no crucial task slips through the cracks.

As an entrepreneur, time is your most valuable asset. The checklist becomes your compass, guiding you through the maze of responsibilities, appointments, and tasks. Its power lies not just in its simplicity, but in its ability to transform scattered moments into a coherent narrative of efficiency.

The Alarm of Accountability: A Timekeeper for Success

In the dynamic world of entrepreneurship, every moment counts. Setting an alarm serves as a subtle reminder of the promises you've made to yourself. It becomes the timekeeper, nudging you towards achieving each goal on your checklist. This disciplined approach ensures that your time is utilized with precision and purpose.

Closing the Week:
A Reflection on Accomplishments

In essence, the Sunday ritual of preparing for the week becomes a cornerstone of your success. As Friday arrives, take a moment to reflect on the week's accomplishments. This practice not only solidifies the habit but also sets the tone for a continuous cycle of purposeful weeks.

Master Your Mondays, Conquer Your Week
Mastering Mondays isn't just a routine, it's a mindset. Embrace this intentional approach, and witness how each Monday sets the tone for a week filled with achievements, efficiency, and a sense of accomplishment. As you conquer each Monday, you pave the way for a journey where purpose becomes the driving force behind your entrepreneurial success.

EXPANDING HORIZONS: THE PROFITABLE REALM OF DIGITAL ADVERTISING BOARDS

Unlock a new revenue stream within your business by delving into the world of digital advertising boards, also known as TV screens. This dynamic tool allows you to showcase visual slides, digital business cards featuring QR codes, and promotional content, transforming idle moments into opportunities for engagement. The key to generating income lies in persuading your clients to run ads on your digital board, creating a symbiotic relationship that benefits both parties.

Imagine your waiting area becoming a hub of resources, providing customers with engaging content while they await your services. This initiative not only fosters a sense of community but also positions your business as a hub of valuable information. Establishing analytics to track monthly and yearly traffic to your business becomes crucial for evaluating the impact of your digital advertising efforts.

Visibility is a cornerstone of success, and if your business performs 20,000 services a year, you possess a powerful leverage point. Utilize this robust book of business as a form of advertising. Invest in a 55-inch digital advertising screen and offer ad slots ranging from $30 to $100 per month. As your book of business fills up, explore different tier levels, each priced for a specific exposure level.

The beauty of this strategy lies in its scalability. Build a substantial book of business through ads, creating a referral powerhouse. People inherently seek referrals, especially from trusted sources. By positioning yourself as a reliable figure, you become the go-to recommendation, establishing your business as a no-brainer choice for those in your community.

In embracing the digital advertising board, you're not just investing in a screen, you're unlocking a gateway to a thriving community and additional income. This innovative approach transforms idle moments into opportunities, propelling your business to new heights through strategic visibility and community building. Elevate your business game and witness the transformative power of thoughtful engagement and profitability.

EXPANSION: BUILDING LAYERS FOR BUSINESS SUCCESS

As you navigate the journey of entrepreneurship, remember to continually expand vertically within your business. The key lies in diversification—adding layers of complementary products and services to your core business. This strategic approach allows you to scale seamlessly within your existing framework. Whether it's introducing a vending machine, offering branded merchandise like t-shirts and books, or integrating a digital advertising screen, each addition becomes an extension of your brand.

By diversifying, you create a comprehensive brand experience for your customers. The presence of your products and services, whether in-store or through strategic placements, builds lasting brand recognition. This not only enhances customer loyalty but also generates additional sales without having to step outside your established space.

So, keep growing vertically, layer by layer, and watch your business flourish with newfound depth and resonance. Your brand is more than a transaction, it's a dynamic, evolving entity that leaves a lasting imprint in the minds of your audience. Elevate your business by continually adding value and relevance, and let the layers you build become the pillars of your success.

THE GIRAFFE & TURTLE CONVERSATION

In the intricate dance of life, imagine a dialogue between a giraffe and a turtle—a fascinating interplay of perspectives where two beings with vastly different viewpoints communicate. Similarly, what feels ordinary to you might be an unknown territory for others. The range of options you see may be out of reach for someone else. Comfort zones and risk tolerance, like the ebb and flow of the tides, differ among individuals. And that, unequivocally, is perfectly okay.

Always remember, you are the embodiment of someone's wildest dreams. Whether a business is calling your name, a destination is beckoning your exploration, or a coveted car awaits you, seize the opportunities. You are the master of your destiny, serving yourself in ways no one else can. Life is a fleeting journey, and in embracing activities that propel the best version of yourself, you create a symphony of experiences.

For those who cast doubt or fear, pay them no heed. In the vast mosaic of existence, weave the threads of your dreams and aspirations. Be the entrepreneur, traveler, or car enthusiast you envision. Don't let the hesitations of others dim the unique light that defines you. Life unfurls its truest beauty as you navigate the path to your authentic self. Rise above the whispers of doubt, spread your wings, and soar. Embrace your dreams and let your melody resonate through the realms of possibility.

RESPECT

VALUE

TRUST

LOVE

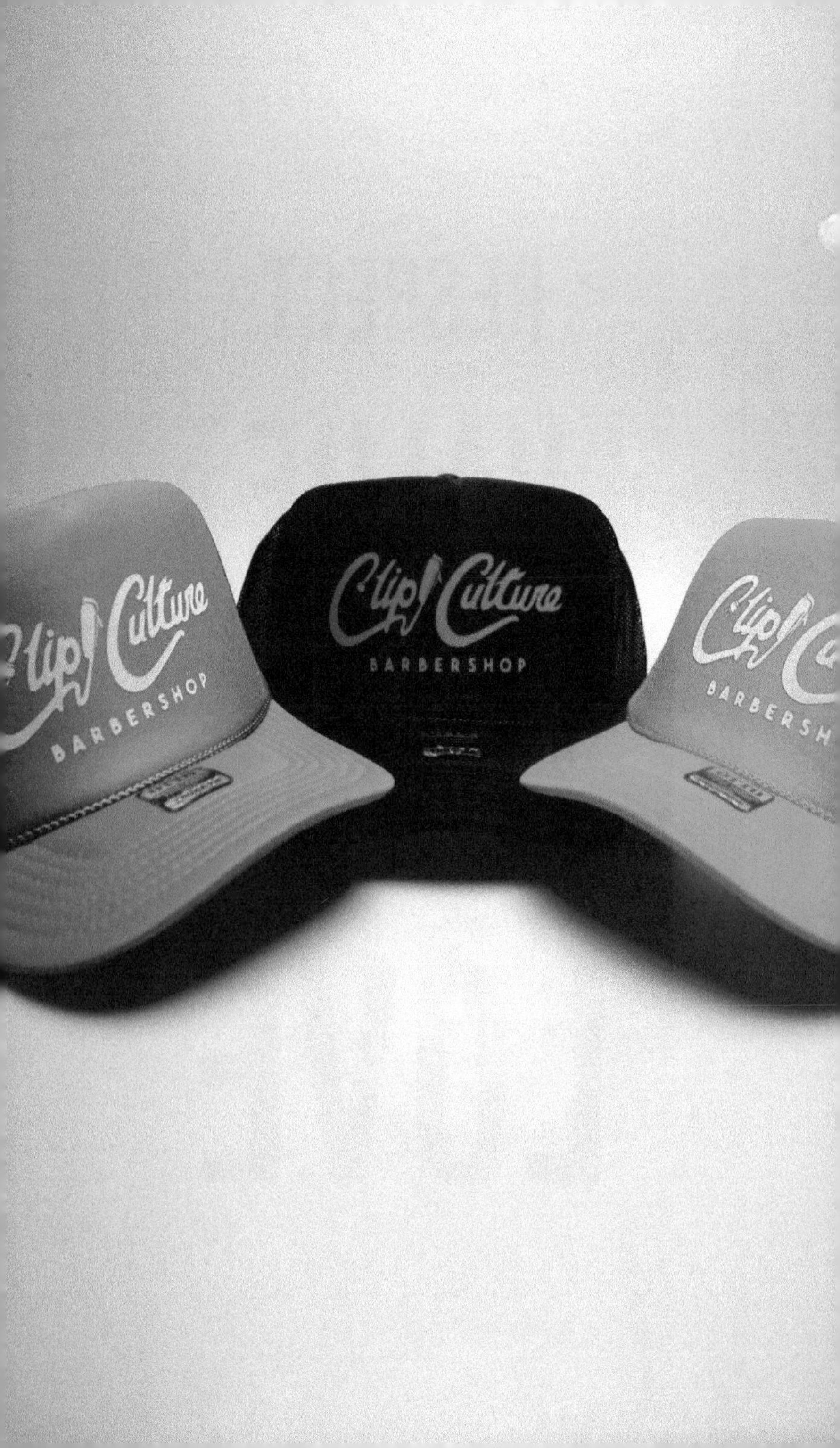
Clip Culture
BARBERSHOP

NO ODOR, NO PROBLEM: BUSINESS HYGIENE ESSENTIALS

As you step into the dynamic realm of business, equipped with strategy and intellect, there's an often-overlooked aspect that wields significant influence—personal hygiene. Bad hygiene isn't just a faux pas, it's a potential deal-breaker that can swiftly remove opportunities from the negotiating table. The unspoken truth is clear—no one is willing to tolerate the discomfort that accompanies poor hygiene practices.

Identifiable traits of bad hygiene encompass a range of factors, from unpleasant breath and lingering weed smoke residue to sweaty body odor, dirty fingernails, and unkempt hair. Such manifestations are a direct reflection of a conscious or inadvertent neglect of one's cleanliness and health requirements. In the business community where trust is paramount, maintaining impeccable hygiene is not just a preference, it's a professional obligation.

Consider this: if a potential business partner can't trust you to uphold basic daily hygiene, how can they trust you with more significant responsibilities? Professionalism is an all-encompassing trait, and the vast majority of individuals shy away from dealings that involve unpleasant body odors or a lack of cleanliness.

Preventing bad hygiene is a proactive choice that can make or break a business interaction. Daily showers, a consistent application of deodorant and cologne within reach, and a travel-friendly kit containing chewing gum, toothpaste, and floss are simple yet effective measures to stay prepared and aware.

In conclusion, navigating the intricate landscape of business demands more than just business acumen—it requires a commitment to professional hygiene. Be a stalwart ambassador of cleanliness, demonstrating that you take your own well-being seriously. In doing so, you pave the way for trust, respect, and successful business dealings.

LOCAL LOVE: CULTIVATING COMMUNITY SUPPORT FOR YOUR BUSINESS

Supporting local businesses is more than a trend, it's a movement, and it's crazy good. Customers crave the familiarity of their local spot—the place where everybody knows your name. It's more than a business, it's a haven, a country club where everyone belongs. Your local business isn't just a place, it's a vibe that draws people in.

Get your merchandise and products into the hands of your clients, and let them become ambassadors for your brand. The word-of-mouth marketing in a tight-knit community is like wildfire—it spreads fast, and it keeps on going. Imagine the pride of seeing your community using your products and talking about your business. It's not just about commerce, it's about building a unique identity that resonates with your community.

In the hustle and bustle of the city, local businesses stand as beacons of community and connection. When your brand becomes an integral part of your customers' lives, it's not merely about business, it's a testament to the local love that fuels your journey. Embrace it, nurture it, and watch your business become an indispensable thread in the fabric of the city's heartbeat.

OPPORTUNITY AWAITS: THE POWER OF KEEPING AN OPEN MIND

In the dynamic landscape of urban opportunities, it's vital to withhold judgment until you've experienced the reality. The saying goes, "Don't knock it until you've tried it," and in the world of business, this holds true. Before dismissing an idea, venture, or potential investment, immerse yourself in it. Your initial 'no' might transform into a resounding 'yes' once you've seen and felt it firsthand.

Whether it's a business venture, a real estate property, or a potential investment, don't let preconceived notions dictate your decisions. Take the time to visit, explore, and understand the context. Sometimes, what appears unattainable becomes a perfect fit once you've given it a chance.

In the urban jungle of opportunities, the key to success lies in keeping an open mind. What might seem out of reach could transform into the perfect venture when you experience it firsthand. Trust your instincts, take that closer look, and let the city reveal its hidden gems. After all, in the landscape of possibilities, saying 'yes' begins with seeing the potential behind every opportunity.

IN FULL STRIDE:
CULTIVATING MOMENTUM FOR SUCCESS

Embarking on the journey of life in full stride is a testament to significant accomplishments and a promising future. It goes beyond mere speed. It's about navigating the twists and turns with purpose and determination. Picture yourself in an apartment you've secured, a space that reflects your independence and growth. Owning a car not only symbolizes mobility but also stands as a tangible reminder of your ability to navigate the roads of life.

As you step into the realm of career-building, you're not just clocking in, you're crafting a path that aligns with your aspirations. This is the phase where your financial stability extends beyond meeting basic needs – it enables you to support your lifestyle and pursue personal passions.

The momentum you've cultivated is more than a series of achievements, it's a narrative of resilience and progress. With your own space, reliable transportation, and a burgeoning career, you're not just moving through life, you're creating a story of success. May this momentum continue propelling you toward greater heights, marking each stride as a testament to your journey's remarkable evolution.

ESSENTIALS OF A GROWN MAN: BUILDING BLOCKS FOR LIFE'S JOURNEY

Every grown man navigates life's complexities armed with a unique set of essentials. These aren't simply possessions, they're the pillars that bolster a man's confidence and provide support in various realms. Here are the six indispensable elements every grown man should have:

1. **Mentorship:** A wise man once said, "Surround yourself with those on the same mission as you." A mentor serves as a guiding light, offering insights and wisdom from a seasoned perspective. Having someone to share experiences and provide guidance is invaluable on life's journey.

2. **Financial Advisor:** Managing finances is a crucial skill, and a financial advisor becomes a trusted ally in this endeavor. From investments to budgeting, having a financial expert ensures that your financial ship sails smoothly through the unpredictable waters of life.

3. **Local Gym Membership:** Physical well-being is the cornerstone of a fulfilling life. A local

gym provides not only a space for physical exercise but also a community that fosters discipline and commitment to a healthy lifestyle.

4. **Therapist:** Mental health is as vital as physical health. A therapist becomes the sounding board for a man's thoughts, helping navigate the complexities of the mind and emotions. It's a proactive step toward holistic well-being.

5. **Nice Car:** While material possessions don't define a man, a reliable and aesthetically pleasing car is more than a mode of transportation. It's a symbol of personal achievements and a testament to one's journey.

6. **Good Woman by His Side:** A supportive partner is a cornerstone of a man's emotional strength. A good woman stands by your side, offering companionship, understanding, and love. Together, you weather life's storms and celebrate its victories.

As you build your arsenal of essentials, remember that the strength of a man is not measured solely by possessions but by the quality of his character and the connections he fosters. Surround yourself with those who uplift and guide you, for in their company, you find the strength to become the best version of yourself.

THE ESSENCE OF RELATIONSHIPS: RESPECT, VALUE, TRUST, & LOVE

I n the intricate dance of relationships, whether within the realm of business or on a personal level, a foundational understanding is paramount. This understanding is encapsulated in four pivotal elements: **Respect, Value, Trust, & Love.**

Respect, the Cornerstone, serves as the bedrock, the fundamental building block upon which all relationships stand. It is the acknowledgment of the inherent worth and dignity of individuals, laying the groundwork for a connection to flourish.

Moving beyond respect, the next layer is **Value, the Recognition of Worth**. When someone or something is deemed valuable, it becomes an asset—a contributor to the relationship's richness. This phase involves recognizing the unique contributions and significance that each element brings.

As the relationship deepens, **Trust, the Bridge of Reliability**, emerges as a crucial bridge. It involves judgment, an assessment of reliability and consistency over time. Trust is earned, and as it solidifies, it becomes the backbone of a relationship's stability.

Positioned as the final layer is **Love, the Culmination.** While a powerful force, it's acknowledged as the last piece of the puzzle. Love, in isolation, can be deceiving. It doesn't pay bills, eliminate envy, or guarantee respect. Love, when built on the foundation of respect, value, and trust, transforms into a force that enriches and strengthens the relationship.

In essence, managing relationships through the lens of **respect** lays the groundwork for a thriving connection. By prioritizing these foundational elements, everything else falls into place. As you navigate the complex tapestry of relationships, remember that **respect is the compass** guiding you through the intricacies of value, trust, and, ultimately, love.

Finally, In the symphony of relationships, the melody of **respect harmonizes with the chords of value, trust, and love, creating a masterpiece that transcends the ordinary**. As you embark on your relational journey, let respect be the guiding star, leading you to connections that are profound, enduring, and transformative.

READ THE ROOM: FOSTERING HARMONY IN COMMUNAL SPACES

In the bustling world of communal spaces, mastering the art of reading the room is a skill that transcends mere observation—it's a key to unlocking success. Picture a dynamic co-working environment, a melting pot of diverse individuals bringing their unique vibes to the table.

Here's the real talk: awareness matters. When you step into this communal symphony, be conscious of your surroundings. Recognize that each person in the room contributes a unique note to the symphony of ideas and work styles. Keeping it on neutral ground, maintaining professionalism—these are the keys to orchestrating harmony.

A casual comment might seem innocuous to you, but in the eyes of others, it could be a decisive note in the composition of your business's reputation. If it's not positively contributing, it might be best to keep it to yourself. In the business arena, your reputation is a precious asset, and every interaction is a brushstroke on the canvas of your establishment.

Your business is not just a provider of products or services. It's an experience. Every conversation, every interaction, shapes the ambiance and determines whether people want to return. There's a time for banter, but mastering the art of reading the room tells you when to hit the right notes.

Imagine yourself as the conductor of this communal symphony, navigating social dynamics with finesse. It's not about being a participant, it's about contributing positively to the shared space. Your awareness, professionalism, and respect for diverse dynamics ensure that your presence enhances the communal experience.

In conclusion, as you navigate the vibrant tapestry of shared spaces, remember the essence of reading the room. Stay neutral, keep it professional, and let your presence be a valuable asset. "Read the Room" is not just a mantra—it's a guide to fostering harmony in communal spaces, ensuring that your business becomes a place where people genuinely want to return.

NAVIGATING THE GRIND: CONQUERING FATIGUE AND STRESS AS AN ENTREPRENEUR

In the relentless hustle of entrepreneurship, where every day feels like a non-stop rollercoaster, fatigue and stress become unwelcome companions. The service business demands resilience, but recognizing when the weight is too heavy is a critical skill that separates endurance from burnout.

Let's cut to the chase—managing fatigue and stress isn't a luxury, it's a survival skill. The workload varies from person to person, and feeling the pressure build up is the signal to hit pause. Ignoring these signs can lead to a cascade of bad decisions—unhealthy eating, questionable financial choices, and a shift in attitude that impacts both you and your business.

Real talk: taking a break is not a sign of weakness,

it's a necessity. Adequate rest is the foundation on which resilience is built. It's about recognizing that your well-being is a non-negotiable component of your business's success. Incorporate regular workouts, stay hydrated, and infuse moments of prayer or meditation throughout the day to center yourself.

Remember, mental health days aren't an indulgence. They're a lifeline. In the fast-paced world of entrepreneurship, where burnout is a looming threat, these days off can save your life and preserve your well-being for the long haul.

In essence, prioritizing self-care isn't simply an act of kindness to yourself. It's a strategic move that fortifies your business. Your well-being is not a secondary concern, it's the bedrock on which your entrepreneurial journey rests. So, embrace those breaks, prioritize self-care, and let your business thrive on the foundation of a resilient and well-balanced entrepreneur.

TIME CRAFT: NAVIGATING THE ENTREPRENEURIAL CLOCK WITH PRECISION

Efficiency is the linchpin of a successful entrepreneurship journey. Messing up preplanned appointments is a surefire way to lose customers, and as independent entrepreneurs, organizing our business is the key to sustaining it for the long haul. The secret sauce? Efficiency.

In the entrepreneurial world, time is a currency, and maximizing your day requires a well-thought-out schedule. Organizing your life and business is about creating a healthy structural balance. Efficiency becomes the silent partner that manages how your day starts and ends. While occasional hiccups are inevitable, having a solid system in place allows you to optimize your time and accomplish more.

Small business success hinges on professionalism, customer service, and, most importantly, efficiency. Consumers crave convenience—they want what they need promptly and efficiently. Providing clients with excellent service, delivering what they want, and ensuring they get their money's worth creates a recipe for endless client retention.

So, fellow entrepreneur, it's time to master the clock, seize the day, and let efficiency be your guiding light. The key to your success lies in giving your clients not just a service but an experience—one they won't forget.

REVITALIZING VIBES: THE POWER OF EMBRACING THE YOUTH MOVEMENT

Starting a new business demands a fresh approach—an infusion of new ideas, perspectives, and boundless creativity. Enter the youth movement, a revolutionary force that brings not only innovation but a renewed sense of joy and energy. In the pursuit of longevity, hitting the refresh button becomes essential.

As a business owner navigating the path of sustainability, it's crucial to recognize when the weight of older perspectives begins to wear you down. Sometimes, hitting the reset and embracing the youth movement is the key to unlocking groundbreaking success. Clean house, make room for new energy, and welcome in a generation between 21-30 eager for fresh opportunities.

This youthful cohort possesses a keen eye for trends, a pulse on global happenings, and, most importantly, the readiness to apply this knowledge. Going younger is more than a strategy, it's a transformative approach to aligning your business with the dynamic currents of the contemporary world.

Don't shy away from making space for the enthusiasm, creativity, and tech-savviness that the youth movement brings. Unlike their more seasoned counterparts who might be stuck in their ways, this fresh wave of talent is poised to elevate your business and propel it into the future.

In the ever-evolving landscape of entrepreneurship, the youth movement isn't just a trend, it's a strategic decision. Embrace the vibrancy of new ideas, the pulse of the younger generation, and watch as your business not only stays afloat but surges ahead with renewed vitality.

NAVIGATING ENDINGS: HONORING THE EXPERIENCE

In the unpredictable journey of life and business, not every connection will stand the test of time, and that's perfectly fine. The key is to honor the experience, even when farewells are inevitable. By doing so, you release the weight of grudges, allowing you to rest easy at night. Every connection had its moment—a time for joy, growth, and shared experiences.

Recognizing that not every relationship is meant to last forever is a liberating perspective. Endings don't have to be laden with hard feelings. They can be transitions, chapters closing to make way for new beginnings. Embracing this mindset allows you to move forward freely, unburdened by the weight of unresolved emotions.

In the tapestry of life, experiences become your guiding stars. When you encounter new faces that echo the past, it's not about dwelling on what was lost but about navigating with the wisdom gained. It's about living off the richness of experience, moving forward with a clearer vision.

Sometimes, things won't end the way you'd hope. Maturity levels differ, and not everyone will handle partings gracefully. Yet, in those moments, honor the experience for what it was—a shared journey that shaped both parties. Living long enough may cast you as the "bad guy," and that's okay. You can't please everyone, but you can choose to honor the richness of every encounter.

In essence, navigating endings is about embracing the ebb and flow of relationships. It's about acknowledging that each connection, whether brief or enduring, contributes to the mosaic of your life. So, honor the experience, cherish the lessons, and stride confidently into the uncharted territories that await.

CAPTURING THE CLIMB: CHRONICLES OF ENTREPRENEURSHIP

In the age of information and the dominance of content, documenting your business journey is a strategic move in the playbook of success. We're living in the Content Era, where every step, every triumph, and every lesson learned can be shared and cherished. For an entrepreneur, this isn't only about self-reflection. It's about offering a guiding light to those who aspire to tread the same path.

Imagine turning your business journey into a captivating docuseries—a visual narrative that unravels the intricacies of starting and structuring a business. This isn't a self-indulgent endeavor. It's a valuable resource for the eager minds craving insight into the entrepreneurial world. By hiring a videographer to capture this odyssey, you're telling a story while creating an educational masterpiece.

This docuseries showcases your successes and pulls back the curtain on the challenges, pitfalls, and unexpected discoveries. It's about providing a real, unfiltered look into what it takes to navigate the entrepreneurial landscape. Break the film into segments and offer different tiers or subscription levels. It becomes a tool that can save aspiring entrepreneurs money, offering a practical understanding of the process.

As the business owner, this journey becomes your leverage—a means to not only share your experiences but to charge for your valuable insights. Demonstrate your success and showcase the grace with which you maneuver through challenges. Reveal the boss moves, the behind-the-scenes hustle, and the sheer determination it takes to get things done.

Our community needs to see what success looks like, and more importantly, how to achieve it. By transforming your startup journey into a documented saga, you're not just building a brand, you're becoming a beacon of inspiration. So, embark on this visual odyssey, capture the climb, and let the world witness the real, unfiltered journey of an entrepreneur getting shit done!

THE LOVE BLUEPRINT: STRATEGIES FOR CHOOSING YOUR RIDE OR DIE

In the unpredictable journey of love, choosing a life partner is a decision that requires more than fleeting emotions. It's about marrying where you're headed, not just where you stand. Take a moment to reflect deeply before taking the leap, avoiding permanent decisions based on temporary feelings.

Maintaining control over your choices is crucial. While feelings are important, a successful union goes beyond emotions. Avoid the trap of two financially challenged individuals forming a non-profit organization. The key is to marry up—find someone equally yoked to your ambitions, someone who complements and supports your endeavors.

Seek a partner who not only meets your criteria but

also adds an extra layer of interest and intrigue to your life. Being with someone inspiring and compatible prevents the draining task of constantly elevating your partner to your level. Remember, you can do bad all by yourself.

Create a criteria list for the partner you envision and frequent events where like-minded individuals gather. In your quest for the right spouse, don't forget to seek guidance from a higher power. While perfection may be elusive, giving yourself the best chance at love and a successful marriage starts with intentional choices.

As you navigate the path to a lasting union, remember that the journey is as significant as the destination. In the dance of love, make moves that align with the partner you're becoming, not just the person you are now.

ERA OF WEALTH AND CHOICES: NAVIGATING THE SHIFT IN MINDSET

In the dynamic landscape of 2023 and beyond, we find ourselves immersed in the era of money and options. It's a paradigm shift from the days of building and growing, a testament to the evolving mindset of our society. In major cities, the pervasive influence of the Money and Options era is palpable, and patience seems to be in short supply.

Generations change every 25 years, and with it, the lens through which we view success transforms. The traditional notion of staying down until you come up, synonymous with the old-school ethos, clashes with the contemporary mantra of getting what you can, as quickly as you can. While building and growing still hold relevance, the Money and Options era prioritizes speed and immediate gains.

The challenge lies in the thin line between calculated moves and impulsive decisions. The allure of swift success can be enticing, but the pitfalls become evident when the tide turns unfavorably. It's a revolving door where bouncing from one idea to the next becomes the norm. The job market reflects this, with a plethora of undeveloped individuals who jump ship too quickly, missing out on the opportunity to hone real-life skills.

Finding your niche, allowing your skills to manifest, requires a discerning approach. The Money and Options mindset, while promising quick wins, may hinder the discovery of your true potential. True growth is not about doing things because you can. It's about making wise decisions that stand the test of time. In this ever-evolving landscape, understanding the delicate balance between speed and sustainability becomes the key to navigating the era of wealth and choices.

LEGACY BUILDING: BEYOND THE MOMENT

In the hustle of life, there's a call to transcend the immediate gains of money or the fervor of love. It's a call to create a legacy that echoes through time, a legacy woven into the fabric of your last name. Your family's surname is a foundation upon which you stand. Building a legacy isn't about fleeting accomplishments. It's about the enduring impact of events, actions, and the essence of your life.

Let's be real—legacy goes beyond what you leave behind for yourself. It's also about what you leave for generations to come. It's about crafting a narrative that extends far beyond your years, resonating in the stories told to your kids, their kids, and beyond. The true measure of success lies not only in what you amass during your journey but in the legacy that outlives you.

So, as you navigate the intricacies of life, keep an eye on the bigger picture. What you do today is a brushstroke in the masterpiece of your legacy. Whether it's a business, a philosophy, or a way of life, ensure it's something that can withstand the test of time. In the grand scheme of things, creating a legacy that extends three generations deep is the ultimate accomplishment—one that speaks volumes about the richness of your life's work.

REFLECTIONS: A REALITY CHECK

I n the realm of self-perception, it's easy to succumb to the allure of an inflated sense of self. No one wants to be the smartest person in the room, but often, individuals overestimate their value in various aspects of life—be it in business, personal relationships, or politics. It's a subtle form of narcissism, and the truth is, most people around you might not share the same perspective.

Here's a real talk exercise: ask 10 friends or family members to share their candid thoughts about you, and here's the kicker—don't respond. Just listen. It's not about seeking validation or affirmation. It's about gaining genuine insights. As you collect their responses, pay attention to any recurring themes. Do certain aspects stand out? Are there areas where you could improve or develop further?

The beauty of this exercise lies in its raw honesty. It's an opportunity for self-reflection, a chance to bridge the gap between who you believe you are in your head and how others perceive you. After all, personal growth is a continuous journey, and understanding your strengths, weaknesses, opportunities, and threats is the cornerstone of meaningful development.

So, embrace this exercise as a reality check—a mirror that reflects not only who you think you are but also the nuanced layers that others see. It's a pathway to self-discovery, a tool for personal development, and a genuine step towards becoming the best version of yourself.

A HUSTLER AIN'T SHIT IF HE CAN'T SAVE.

OWNING MY JOURNEY: THE POWER OF RESPONSIBILITY

I n the journey of self-discovery, one undeniable truth stands tall—I am the architect of my own destiny. The messiness in my work, the moments of misbehavior—they are not dictated by external forces but are products of my choices. It's a crucial realization that shifts the narrative from blaming others to embracing responsibility for my actions.

Every misstep is an opportunity for growth, a chance to refine and improve. Blaming external circumstances only serves as a distraction from the true essence of accountability. It's time to shed the cloak of excuses and stand bare, facing the mirror of self-reflection. The choices I make shape the person I become, and responsibility is the linchpin of my success.

No longer can I attribute my actions to external factors. I am who I am because of the decisions I make. It's a liberating acknowledgment that places the reins of my journey firmly in my hands. If success is the destination, responsibility becomes the compass guiding my path. In this narrative, "If it is up to me, it is up to me!" echoes as a powerful mantra—a reminder that my destiny lies within my grasp, shaped by the responsibility I choose to embrace.

Personal Responsibility Charter

Respect	Trustworthy	Responsibility
• Treat others with Respect • Be tolerant of differences • Maintain good manners and avoid bad language • Refrain from threatening, hitting, or hurting anyone • Handle anger, insults, and disagreements peacefully	• Be honest • Avoid deception, cheating, or stealing • Demonstrate reliability; Do what you say you will do • Have the courage to do the right thing • Build a good reputation • Be loyal and stand by your family, friends, and faith	• Fulfill your obligations • Persevere: Keep on trying • Exercise self-control • Be self-disciplined • Think before you act; consider the consequences • Be accountable for your choices

EMBRACING REJECTION: THE POWER OF A NO

I n the entrepreneurial journey, hearing a "no" can be the catalyst for growth and success. Contrary to disappointment, a "no" is not the end. It's an opportunity to reassess, recalibrate, and rise above. Imagine a world where every "no" is viewed not as a roadblock but as a stepping stone to realizing your full potential. It's in the face of rejection that creativity is unleashed, determination is tested, and the grind is amplified.

Receiving a "no" is a pivotal moment, a crossroads where you decide whether to accept defeat or innovate. Dissatisfaction with a "no" becomes the driving force behind finding alternative solutions. As an entrepreneur, it's a call to go harder, grind smarter, and prove that setbacks are merely setups for comebacks.

This is the paradox of rejection—it's not a setback but a setup for something better. Each "no" is a divine intervention, saving you from potential pitfalls and guiding you toward a more prosperous path. In the realm of entrepreneurship, a "no" is not a closed door. It's an invitation to explore new avenues, uncover hidden potentials, and align with a destiny far grander than you envisioned.

So, the next time you face rejection, don't let discouragement take root. Instead, see it as a divine redirection, a cosmic affirmation that something better awaits. Embrace the power of "no," for within its resistance lies the resilience that propels you toward unparalleled success.

DIGITAL HUSTLE: AIR DROP YOUR WAY TO SUCCESS

In the dynamic landscape of entrepreneurship, staying ahead means embracing technology's transformative power. Bid farewell to the traditional business card and welcome the era of air dropping your digital calling card. Imagine effortlessly connecting with potential clients, bypassing the awkwardness of face-to-face exchanges. This modern approach not only simplifies the networking game but also opens doors to new opportunities in the digital realm.

For those entrepreneurs who navigate the business

world with a hint of social anxiety or prefer a more streamlined strategy, air dropping is a game-changer. As you stroll through the mall or navigate daily life, seize the chance to digitally share your business with potential clients. Adapt to the times, make networking more accessible, and witness the impact of a tech-savvy approach on your entrepreneurial journey. Try it out, and watch as your business connects with the future.

TIMING IS EVERYTHING: THE ART OF SCALING RIGHT

In the dynamic world of business, the temptation to scale quickly is ever-present. But here's the real talk. Scaling too fast can be a recipe for disaster. It's like sprinting before you've learned to walk. The result is often a stumble. Quality work is the backbone of any successful enterprise, and rushing the scaling process can jeopardize that foundation.

Let's break it down: timing is everything. Instead of sprinting toward growth, consider a strategic and vertical approach. Build your business from within, enhancing products, services, and promotions. It's like laying a strong foundation before constructing the next floor. Rushing this process can lead to poor-quality output, tarnishing your hard-earned reputation.

Reputation is the currency of business, and once it takes a hit, the road to recovery is steep. Bad press is like a stain that's hard to wash off. You must meet demand and exceed expectations. So, grow smart from within, add layers thoughtfully, and when the time is right, scale with precision. Remember, it's not about how fast you go. It's about how well you navigate the journey.

TWO
BROKE
PEOPLE TOGETHER
IS A
NONPROFIT
ORGANIZATION

BECOMING TOMORROW:
THE DAILY RENT OF SUCCESS

Here's the raw truth: what you're going to be is embedded in what you're becoming right now, in the hustle and grind of today. Success isn't a one-time payment, it's a daily rent, and you've got to show up, wallet in hand, every single day. The light at the end of the tunnel might seem dim, but your focus is the key to amplifying it.

What you want to become isn't a distant dream. Rather, it's a daily grind. Success demands more than wishes. It craves dedication, determination, and a hunger for knowledge and experience. Nothing is beyond your reach, no goal is off-limits, but it all boils down to how hard you're willing to go. Your destiny isn't written in the stars. It's crafted by the choices you make every day.

The truth is, if you don't get where you want to go, the blame falls on your shoulders. You're not held back by external forces. You are your own superpower. So, as you navigate the journey to your aspirations, remember that success isn't a far-off destination. It's a daily commitment. The rent is due every day, and the key to unlocking your tomorrow is in the actions you take today.

OPPORTUNITY KNOCKS, BUT HOW FAR?

Let's talk real talk here: sometimes, the fine line between something being the right fit and it falling apart is the geographical gap. You might vibe with someone, or a job might seem tailor-made for you, but the distance becomes the invisible barrier that holds you back. However, let's not get it twisted. Loyalty to convenience can trap you in a cycle you don't want.

Here's the deal: it all has to make sense. When you come across an opportunity that aligns with your gut feeling, it's time to assess. Break it down—weigh the pros and cons. Ask yourself the tough questions: Is it worth the risk? What do I stand to lose, and what's the gain? Sometimes, the distance clouds your vision, and you need to cut through the fog.

When in doubt, follow your heart, but don't forget the power of prayer. Take a step back, fast for a few days, and let the answers come to you. The journey must make sense in the grand scheme of things. As you navigate the geography of opportunities, keep in mind that it's not just about the destination, it's about the journey that makes sense in your story.

THE RHYTHM OF WEALTH: MAKING CASH FLOW MOVES

In the symphony of financial success, the drumbeat that sets the pace is cash flow. Business owners must orchestrate a wave that keeps the currency flowing in. Real estate, a classic player in this financial melody, builds wealth and equity, but it's often a slow dance. Unless you've got a construction team flipping houses at lightning speed, the growth takes time.

Cash flow is about continuous streams of income. Cash reigns supreme, and examples of businesses that create instant cash flow are scattered across the landscape. Think lawn care, cleaning services, car washes, laundromats, barbershops, hair salons, strip clubs, vending machines, ATMs—the list goes on.

So, the key? Secure yourself a business that injects positive cash flow into your pockets. Be the maestro of your financial symphony, conducting the rhythm of income. Once you've mastered the beat, it's time to consider building that real estate portfolio. It's about creating a financial composition that stands the test of time.

THE TAP OUT BUTTON: TAKING OWNERSHIP IN BUSINESS

In the arena of business, there's a phenomenon known as the "Tap Out Button." It's the moment when someone, once thriving in your business or under your guidance, points fingers when the going gets tough. When the cash flow is steady, and victories are in abundance, all is well. But the real character shows when the tide shifts.

Here's the real talk: blaming the leader when the money train slows down is the easy way out. True growth comes from within, acknowledging shortcomings, and learning to navigate the challenges. No leader can carry you forever. They can teach you how to fish, but it's on you to cast your own line. Be a self-starter. Get things done.

A good leader positions you to win, but the responsibility to sustain that success lies with the individual. It's a simple equation: Learn, then Earn. If a leader opens doors for you, it doesn't mean you become dependent on them for a lifetime. The key to long-term success is self-sufficiency. Keep it simple, take ownership, and thrive independently.

ELEVATE YOUR HUSTLE: THE ART OF DELEGATION IN BUSINESS

Embarking on the entrepreneurial journey is no walk in the park, especially during those crucial first 3-5 years. As the business owner, your presence is vital to keep the ship sailing smoothly. It's the hustle phase, the grind to establish your mark. But here's the real talk: it's a phase, not a forever state.

Once you've weathered the initial storm, it's time for a strategic shift. If your earnings are entangled with the business's struggles, it's a sign. A sign that it's time to work on your business, not just in it. The game plan?

Delegation. Yes, it's an art. Delegating responsibilities becomes the mantra for evolution. It's about formulating a plan that allows you to pass the torch to others, empowering them to take charge.

Remember, the motto is simple but profound: Delegate, then Elevate. It's not just about the growth of your business, about the growth of your entrepreneurial journey. So, take that step, master the art of delegation, and watch as your business not only survives but thrives in your absence. Elevate your hustle to a new level of success.

POOR MOUTHING CHRONICLES: DECODING MANIPULATION IN LIFE

In the game of life, we encounter various players, and some play by using a tactic called poor mouthing. Now, poor mouthing isn't just storytelling. It's a form of manipulation. It's that friend or associate who constantly wants you to feel sorry for them, hoping to score perks or benefits from your sympathy. Real talk: it's a subtle cry for someone else to swoop in and save the day. But here's the truth—only Jesus can save you, not the sympathy of others.

Poor mouthing is a manifestation of a poverty mindset. These folks aren't looking to figure out life for themselves, they're looking for a savior. They'll paint a vivid picture of their struggles, how bad off they are, and, let's be real, nobody wants to hear that. These are the people who stick around as long as you're handing out assistance. The minute you cut them off, they're off to the next source.

So, here's the real talk closer: rise above the game. Recognize poor mouthing for what it is—a manipulation. Don't let sympathy blind you, and don't let someone else's narrative become your responsibility. In the game of life, choose to play with those who uplift, not those who constantly play the victim card.

THRIVING IN THE 3 H'S: A BLUEPRINT FOR A BETTER YOU

I n the journey of life, reaching the seat of Happy, Healed, and Healthy transforms the way you navigate the world. Let's face it, we've all collected a few bumps and bruises along the way, but it's the ones who've done the hard work on themselves that stand out. When you're truly content, emotionally healed, and physically healthy, your demeanor changes. The small stuff doesn't get under your skin. You let life flow.

It's a fact: life throws curveballs, and not everything goes as planned. However, the difference lies in how you handle it. The happy, healed, and healthy approach means you don't unravel at the seams when faced with adversity. It's a state of being that radiates resilience and inner strength. So, embark on the journey of self-discovery, do the work, and embrace the transformative power of the 3 H's. Your happiness, healing, and health are the keys to unlocking a life lived on your terms.

NAVIGATING BUSINESS REALITIES: THE AVERAGE MEDIAN INCOME GUIDE

Entering the business arena requires more than just a dream, it demands a strategic understanding of your surroundings. The average median income becomes your compass, drawing a line that separates the playing field. Imagine it as the pulse of the community—the amount that splits the population into halves, those above and those below. Your business is poised to orbit around this crucial marker, defining the economic landscape.

Now, let's keep it real. Gentrification might alter the game, but for most entrepreneurs, it's about aligning with the current pulse of the community.

Understanding the average median income means recognizing the financial heartbeat of your potential clientele.

As you embark on your business journey, consider the implications of this income divide. Tailor your strategies to resonate with the economic realities of the community. Whether you're establishing a local shop or launching an online venture, acknowledging and working within the framework of the average median income can be the key to unlocking success.

In the realm of business, it's not just about chasing dreams, it's about navigating the practicalities. So, study the figures, embrace the realities, and let the average median income be your guide to sustainable growth.

ELEVATE YOUR TALK: ESCAPING THE TRAP OF LOW VIBRATIONAL CONVERSATIONS

In the world of hustle and grind, the conversations we engage in are more than just words – they're a reflection of our mindset. Low vibrational conversations, those empty exchanges about nothing, have the power to drag you down. It's all about what you feed your mind. Just like junk food affects your body, consuming negativity can mess with your brain.

The key is to be mindful of what you expose yourself to – from what you watch on social media to the music that fuels your vibe.

Let's keep it real. Low vibrational conversations often stem from dysfunction, and in the game of business and management, you can't afford to let that energy seep in. Your circle matters – who you hang around, what you watch, and what you listen to. As an entrepreneur, protecting your business means safeguarding it from the toxicity of low vibrations. If someone brings that negative energy into your space, cut ties swiftly. Don't let a mindset of dysfunction contaminate the thriving environment you've worked hard to build. It's time to elevate your talk, elevate your mindset, and secure success on your own terms.

RISING TOGETHER: ELEVATING YOUR CIRCLE WITH HIGH LEVEL CONVERSATIONS

In the grind of life, conversations can either lift you up or pull you down. High-level conversations? Now, that's where the magic happens. Imagine a crew that not only talks the talk but walks the walk, a squad that fuels your growth and ignites your learning. These are the people who've tasted success, traveled the world, embraced culture, and soaked in education.

If you're aiming high, these are the minds you need around you. High-level individuals illuminate, inspire, and push you to surpass your limits. Their thinking? It's broad, like the view from the top. When life throws curveballs, these folks come armed with solutions. Life's tough no doubt. So, why not surround yourself with the kind of people who not only get it but also uplift you?

Let's keep it real. Finding your tribe is key. Seek out those high-level minds that resonate with your journey. Because in the game of life, you deserve a circle that not only has your back but also propels you forward. It's time to rise together, level up your conversations, and conquer life with a crew that's got your back.

NAVIGATING TOUGH EXITS: THE NEED FOR A POLICE ESCORT

Running a small business comes with its share of challenges, and unfortunately, not every farewell is a peaceful one. Imagine you've gotta let someone go, and suddenly it's not about the pink slip, it's about safety.

We all know not everyone takes a departure gracefully. Some folks might be packing more than just their cubicle knick-knacks. They could be carrying a whole lot of bad energy. As a business owner, your safety comes first. It's not about being paranoid. It's about being smart.

So, what's the move? When it's time to part ways, consider rolling with a police escort. Yeah, it might sound extreme, but it's a real talk necessity. Protect yourself, your business, and let the pros handle the tough situations. Have the cops help them gather their stuff, document the exit, and ensure it's all by the book.

Remember, it's not about playing tough. It's about playing smart. As a business owner, you've got enough on your plate. Let the police handle the exits, so you can focus on steering your business to success.

SPACE MATTERS: NAVIGATING SQUARE FOOTAGE IN BUSINESS

Let's chop it up real about space – wasted square footage is a game-changer, especially when you're laying down the blueprint for your business. Opening a shop? Measure twice, cut once. That extra space might seem fly, but trust, it's gonna hit you where it hurts – your bills.

Counting the Cost: It's All in the Bills

Every inch you're not using is money down the drain. AC bill? Water bill? Electricity? Yeah, they're all looking for a piece of that unused space. Too much room? Your overhead starts feeling like a heavyweight champ, knocking out your hard-earned cash.

Small Moves, Big Vibes

In a world where people want to catch a vibe and bounce, you don't need a space the size of a stadium. Small spots with the right energy can pull in more crowds than you think. Think smart, not big.

Budget Battles: Don't Let Square Footage KO Your Earnings

Too much square footage can bleed your budget dry – we're talking serious cash, maybe even 50k or more.

Your dream spot can turn into a financial nightmare if you're not careful. Choose wisely. Don't let the contractor's build-out budget catch you slipping.

So, when you're plotting your business moves, remember: size matters, but not in the way you might think. Keep it tight, use what you need, and let your space work for you, not against you. The streets respect the ones who move smart.

ROLLING IN SUCCESS: THE MOBILE HUSTLE

L et's talk about getting on the move – mobile services, fam. Whether you're slinging food from a truck, running a mobile barbershop, or hooking up rides with your detail game, it's a solid way to push your brand to the streets. Convenience is the name of the game, and people are willing to pay for it.

Street Smart: Bringing Your Biz to Them
Not everyone can roll up to your spot regularly, but they might catch you on the move. Mobile services break down those barriers. If your game is tight, they'll follow your wheels wherever they go.

Pit Stops: The Cost of the Mobile Grind
Now, let's keep it 100 – mobile life ain't all smooth

cruising. Your ride needs some TLC too – we're talking maintenance, gas, oil changes, new tires, and the regular wear and tear. So, before you hit the road, make sure you're factoring in those travel costs in your business expenses.

Street Deals: Hustling Contracts
You ain't just riding around for kicks. You're securing those contracts. Schools, funeral homes, prisons, private sectors, hospitals—they all need what you're offering. They might not have regular business hours, but you can bring your services straight to their doorsteps.

The Roll Call: Advertise on the Move
Mobile services are about pushing your brand. Your wheels become your billboard, and every street you hit

is a new opportunity. It's not just business, it's a lifestyle—moving, grinding, and opening doors for new customers.

So, if you're thinking about taking it to the streets, make sure you're rolling with a plan. Mobile services are a movement. Start the engine, hit the streets, and watch your business go places you never imagined.

STACKING BILLS, BUILDING DREAMS: THE DAILY DOLLAR GAME

In the gritty world of hustling, a true player knows that the game isn't merely about making money, it's about stacking it up. If you're pulling in cash in your hustle, there's no excuse for not having some green saved up. Now, let's break it down for those struggling with the savings game. There are 30 days in a month – simple, right? Here's the hustle: stash a dollar for each day. Day one? Tuck away a crisp buck. Day 30? Slide in a smooth $30. Rinse and repeat. Whether it's a paint bucket, a shoebox, or a secure safe, find your hustle vessel and make it a daily ritual.

Discipline is the key. It's what separates the players from the amateurs. Watch how this small daily grind transforms your financial outlook. Starting small is just the foundation. Soon, you'll be building an empire.

Remember, a true hustler ain't worth a dime if he can't save. Get your hustle on, stack those daily dollars, and watch your game elevate.

HUSTLER'S CHECKLIST: MASTERING SMALL BIZ DUTIES

R unning a small business is a hustle that demands every ounce of your energy. You, as the boss, can't be everywhere at once. It's time to flip the script and create a Duty List for your squad. Divide and conquer – that's the name of the game. There's only so much daylight, and you've got operations to run. Break it down, from cleaning restrooms to handling calls and emails, mopping floors, laundering towels, and taking out the trash – these may be simple tasks, but they're the backbone of your operation.

Here's the real talk: if you've got a team of 7 hustlers, designate each day for a specific duty. It's a standard, a hustle ritual. Whoever can't meet these demands isn't cut out for the game. It's a hustle, and every player needs to pull their weight. If they can't handle the choreography, it's time for them to exit stage left. It's the duty list hustle – where everyone plays a role, or they're out of the show.

MORE

ACTION,

FEWER

ANNOUNCEMENTS.

BEYOND THE BOARDROOM: NURTURING YOUR TEAM'S WELL-BEING

In the hustle and grind of business, it's crucial to remember that your team is more than just cogs in the wheel—they're humans with lives beyond the office walls. Take a beat every 2 or 3 months to do a wellness check on your employees. Beyond the spreadsheets and deadlines, delve into their well-being. Ask about their mental health, and create a space for them to share. There might be questions or family matters lingering, waiting to be addressed.

Understanding your employees on a personal level is the key to unlocking their full potential. Show them you care by simply listening and acknowledging their lives outside of work. Trust is a two-way street, and it starts with demonstrating that you genuinely care. When your team feels valued, productivity soars. So, make it a habit to check in on your employees—because a thriving team means a thriving business.

THREADS OF CONNECTION: NURTURING RELATIONSHIPS THROUGH THE LITTLE THINGS

In the intricate dance of relationships and leadership, it's the little things that weave the fabric of connection. Marriages, friendships, and even business partnerships often crumble not from grand gestures but from the neglect of the small, seemingly inconsequential acts that once built the foundation. The magic is in the details—the surprise notes, the thoughtful gestures, the consistent expressions of care. When these small tokens of affection or appreciation go unresolved, a quiet weight begins to accumulate, and the foundation weakens.

Living intentionally means understanding the gravity of every interaction. As a leader, doing the little things is not just a choice but a responsibility. Lead not just when the spotlight is on, but in those unseen moments. Integrity, the silent force that shapes relationships, lies in the commitment to consistently honor the little things. In the grand tapestry of life, it's the subtle threads that create a masterpiece.

PROGRESSIVE PARTNERSHIPS: CRAFTING A FUTURE BEYOND THE PRESENT

In the intricate dance of relationships and leadership, it's the little things that weave the fabric of connection. Marriages, friendships, and even business partnerships often crumble not from grand gestures but from the neglect of the small, seemingly inconsequential acts that once built the foundation. The magic is in the details—the surprise notes, the thoughtful gestures, the consistent expressions of care. When these small tokens of affection or appreciation go unresolved, a quiet weight begins to accumulate, and the foundation weakens.

Living intentionally means understanding the gravity of every interaction. As a leader, doing the little things is not just a choice but a responsibility. Lead not just when the spotlight is on, but in those unseen moments. Integrity, the silent force that shapes relationships, lies in the commitment to consistently honor the little things. In the grand tapestry of life, it's the subtle threads that create a masterpiece.

BREAKING EVERY CHAIN: NAVIGATING LIFE BEYOND TOXIC BONDS

In the unforgiving tapestry of life, a disturbing phenomenon known as trauma bonding often emerges. This toxic connection is formed when individuals, devoid of meaningful pursuits in their own lives, unite with the sole purpose of casting shadows on your name. They find solidarity in their shared penchant for disparaging you, creating a destructive alliance that thrives on negativity. It's a stark reminder that some people, unable to navigate their own shortcomings, seek solace in dragging others down.

Trauma bonding extends beyond mere verbal attacks. It involves reflecting on past miseries that serve no constructive purpose. The act of dwelling on negative experiences becomes a collective exercise, binding these individuals in a web of shared grievances. The danger lies not only in their attempts to prey on your downfall but also in the mutual reinforcement of toxic narratives.

However, as you navigate the intricacies of life,

remember that you have the power to resist and rise above such destructive dynamics. Instead of succumbing to trauma bonding, channel your energy into forging new solutions. Redirect your focus towards positive endeavors that contribute to personal growth and well-being.

In essence, your journey is about transcending the noise and steering clear of those who revel in perpetuating negativity. By doing so, you reclaim control over your narrative, leaving behind the toxic bonds that threaten to drag you down. It's a testament to your resilience and determination to navigate life's challenges with grace and purpose.

THE LIBERATION CODE: UNLEASHING THE POWER OF LETTING GO

In the grand symphony of life, the melody of liberation plays through the chords of letting go. Clinging onto things, be it toxic relationships or one-sided connections, only weighs us down in the end. It's a paradox—by fearing loss, we often end up losing more. The key is to cut off the dead weight, making room for new possibilities to flow into our lives. Fear is an illusion. Faith is the reality we should operate in.

Letting go is a profound act of self-love and empowerment. It's about releasing the anchors that hold us back and embracing the freedom of new beginnings. The power of letting go is a transformational journey toward a better version of oneself. As you master this power, life becomes a canvas of limitless opportunities, and worries fade away.

Surround yourself with people and experiences that fuel your growth and inspire you to be the best version of yourself. The power of letting go is the gateway to a life where encounters add value and purpose. If it doesn't serve you, it's time to let that go. Embrace the liberation code, and watch as your life transforms into a masterpiece of authenticity and fulfillment.

LINK UP, LEVEL UP: NAVIGATING REAL CONNECTIONS

In a world glued to screens, the real magic of connection often happens outside the glow of smartphones. Ditch the superficial nightclub atmosphere and dive into the real deal—events, house parties, and meet-up groups. These aren't just gatherings, they're the doorways to a world where genuine connections spark and evolve.

During the holidays, swap the ordinary for the extraordinary. Hit up Friendsgiving house bashes or rock the scene at an ugly Christmas sweater party. The goal is to break free from the monotony, mingle with fresh faces, and ride the unpredictable wave of life. Take the plunge into different social groups, each experience a stepping stone to new possibilities.

Trips are mind-expanding journeys. Invest in yourself and embark on three or four trips a year. Venturing into new places allows sightseeing and enables you to broaden your horizons, understand diverse perspectives, and stumble upon someone who might just alter the course of your life.

Now, when it comes to getting social, house parties with games are the hidden gems. Games break the ice, turning strangers into comrades. Unlike the club scene where everyone's frontin', these intimate gatherings foster authentic interactions. So, step out from behind your phone screen, join the movement, and let the real vibes elevate your connections.

CASH RULES EVERYTHING AROUND TRAVEL (C.R.E.A.T.)

Embarking on a journey with someone who's playing hide-and-seek with their wallet? It's a reality check, but folks are really out here thinking they can globe-trot without the cash to back it up. If your pockets are echoing emptiness, it's cool—sit this one out. Nobody's stepping up to bankroll your entire adventure. Get real and plan ahead. Set a budget that respects your finances and the experiences you're craving. Don't be that person nickel-and-diming their way through a trip, squeezing every penny till it screams. Have your funds ready for dinners, Uber rides, thrilling excursions, and don't forget to spread the love with those serving you. Make sure your travel experience is a symphony of unforgettable moments, not a cacophony of financial headaches. Buckle up, budget up, and get ready for a journey worth every penny.

So, before you pack your bags, pack your pockets.

A well-planned adventure is the key to unlocking a world of incredible experiences. Don't be the one stuck counting pennies while others make memories. Travel smart, stack right, and let the good times roll without any fiscal hiccups. Safe travels!

RICH N FIT CHRONICLES: THE BLUEPRINT TO BOSS MOVES

In the hustle game, health is more than a flex. It's the ultimate wealth. Imagine a lifestyle where you're not just rich in the bank but also fit, ready to conquer every avenue life throws at you. It's not about vanity, it's about options, mindset, and boss-level moves. Business owners, listen up – your physical game is as crucial as your financial game. You're constantly on the move, meeting new faces, and navigating a world that demands the best version of you. So, gear up, not just in suits for events but also in a physique that commands attention.

Getting rich is a marathon, not a sprint, demanding discipline and strategy. It's about making those calculated moves that set you apart. Now, let's talk fit. Discipline doesn't discriminate. It's the same force driving financial success and a chiseled physique. Pouring that energy into your body isn't just about aesthetics. It's about sustaining the marathon. Health fuels wealth, and wealth affords the resources to nurture health. It's a cycle of abundance.

So, lace up your financial strategy and your sneakers. Health is the foundation of every boss move you make. Stay rich, stay fit. Beyond a mantra, it's the winning formula for a life that screams success. Time to make those moves, boss. Hustle hard, stay disciplined, and let the world see the rich and fit masterpiece you're creating.

HUSTLE 101:
SORTING THE TALKERS FROM THE DOERS

Homework – it's not just for classrooms. When you're out here making moves and building success, everyone wants a piece of the puzzle. But let's be real, not everyone is cut out for the grind. So, how do you separate the genuine hustlers from the talkers? Easy, you give them homework.

See, it's not about being secretive but about filtering out the noise. People see the glitz, the glam, and the success, but they often forget about the grind, the countless hours, and the struggles behind the scenes. So, when they come knocking, asking for the magic formula, hand them a piece of that grind by giving them homework. It's not a test, it's a reality check.

Success isn't an overnight sensation, it's a symphony of failures, lessons, and relentless effort. For every success story you've crafted, there are years of refining, learning, and mastering the game. The homework is a journey. A curated path to help them understand that success demands work, resilience, and patience.

In a world of instant gratification, the homework strategy is your litmus test for dedication. Click that link in the bio. It's the doorway to the lessons, the struggles, and the victories that shaped your journey. Let the talkers talk. Let the doers do. Homework separates the players from the spectators. Here's to the real hustlers, the ones who put in the work and report back. GAME RECOGNIZES GAME!

RISE AND THRIVE: THE BREAKFAST BLUEPRINT

"**B**reakfast for Champions" is not just a saying. It's a mantra for those navigating the grind. In the concrete jungle, where every move matters, your morning fuel is your secret weapon. Let's break it down. Breakfast sets the stage for a day of domination.

Think of breakfast as the key that starts your hustle engine. You feed your body, spirit, and soul. It's the energy infusion your system craves to kickstart the day in the right direction. In the urban hustle, where every move counts, a good breakfast is your daily investment in success.

But it's not just about preventing mid-morning growls. It's a strategic move. Breakfast becomes your metabolic commander, the guardian of balanced blood sugar, and the patron saint of heart health. It's the energy elixir that propels you through the urban maze. So, before you hit the streets, secure your breakfast for champions.

In a world that never stops moving, breakfast is

your anchor. Don't skip it, savor it. Urban warriors, rise and thrive. Your daily hustle awaits, and it begins with breakfast for champions. Fuel up, lock and load. Success is a breakfast away.

COMMITMENT CHRONICLES: CRAFTING A LIFELONG LOVE STORY

L et's talk marriage – not the glitz and glam of a wedding, but the real deal, the nitty-gritty of a lifetime commitment. In a world where divorce rates loom around 40-50%, it's time to shift our focus from the grandeur of ceremonies to the substance of a lasting union.

When two souls decide to journey together, it's a covenant made in the presence of a higher power. The statistics are out there, and the reasons for divorce vary—infidelity, financial strain, or simply growing apart. Life happens, but that doesn't mean we throw caution to the wind.

So, here's the real talk – plan the marriage, not just the wedding. It's easy to get lost in the aesthetics of a perfect day, but what about the years that follow? What about the moments beyond the honeymoon? These are the questions that matter.

Ask yourself and your partner the hard questions.

Where do you envision your life together? Where do you want to retire? What kind of upbringing do you want for your kids? What's your financial game plan? Which church will be your spiritual home? These are the conversations that lay the foundation for a marriage built to withstand life's storms.

Sure, adjustments will come – that's a given. But having these conversations upfront is the key to resilience. It's about creating a roadmap for a shared life, filled with intentional choices and shared dreams.

So, before you dive into the chaos of wedding planning, take a step back. Look at your partner, see the life you're building together, and plan accordingly. A wedding is a day. A marriage is a lifetime. Let's prioritize the latter. Beyond the aisle lies a journey worth planning for. A marriage that stands the test of time.

CHANGES
START FROM
WITHIN.
NOT BY MOVING
TO ATLANTA.

THE CREATIVITY CODE:
CARVING SPACE IN THE NOISE

In the hustle of life, distractions are like roadblocks that can hinder your journey to success. It's crucial to recognize what truly matters and eliminate anything that doesn't contribute positively to your growth. Cut out the noise, the drama, and the energy-draining situations that only serve as obstacles on your path. Remember, time spent entertaining negativity could be better utilized for cultivating innovative ideas and pushing the boundaries of your potential.

Creating a space free from unnecessary distractions is akin to carving out a sanctuary for your thoughts and creativity. This is where the magic happens – where you can delve into the depths of your mind and pull out groundbreaking concepts. In a world filled with constant chatter and chaos, finding moments of solitude becomes a precious commodity. It's in these moments that you can truly focus on becoming the best version of yourself, nurturing the seeds of innovation that lie within.

So, take the time to pour into yourself, invest in your mental and emotional well-being, and silence the distractions that threaten to drown out your inner voice. Becoming your higher self involves a conscious effort to rise above the noise, to detach from what doesn't serve your purpose, and to embrace a mindset that fosters innovation. In the end, the journey to success is often a journey inward – a process of self-discovery and growth that flourishes in an environment free from unnecessary clutter.

CITY PSALMS: REAL TALK ON FAITHFUL DECISION-MAKING

I n the journey of life, decisions are inevitable, and one must always know that no matter what is happening in life, God is not the author of confusion. This simple yet profound truth resonates with those living intentional lives, where ambiguity has no place. When faced with crossroads, it's essential to pause, reflect, and seek divine guidance. The Creator desires our prosperity and success, and through prayer, we can connect with the divine wisdom that steers us in the right direction.

Drawing inspiration from biblical teachings, consider the words of Proverbs 3:5-6: "Trust in the Lord with all your heart and lean not on your own understanding; in all your ways submit to him, and he will make your paths straight." This scripture emphasizes the importance of trusting God in decision-making, acknowledging that His guidance surpasses our understanding.

Navigating through life requires courage, and making decisions is a testament to that courage. It's about stepping out of comfort zones, trusting the divine plan, and embracing the changes that lead to growth. If clarity eludes you, embark on a 21-day fast – a spiritual journey that not only aligns your spirit but also brings forth the clarity needed for decision-making.

In conclusion, God's guidance is a beacon of light in the midst of confusion. Through prayer, reflection, and faith, we can confidently make decisions that align with our purpose. So, remember, when faced with choices, seek divine intervention, for God is indeed the guiding force in the narrative of our lives.

COMPASSION CHRONICLES: A GIVER'S TALE

In the dynamic tapestry of life, embodying the spirit of generosity is no small accomplishment. It's a distinctive gift that not everyone possesses. This inherent quality presents its own set of challenges, given the diverse array of individuals in the world— some naturally inclined to give, empathizing with the struggles of others, and others predisposed to take without weighing the consequences.

Givers often find themselves at a pivotal juncture, discerning who is genuinely deserving of their generosity and who might become a perpetual drain on their energy. Recognizing that the gift of giving isn't universally applicable is crucial. The world contains individuals who, knowingly or unknowingly, exploit a giver's benevolence. Despite the sincere intention to assist, there comes a juncture where extending a hand may inadvertently foster dependency. Establishing boundaries is not an act of selfishness but a necessary step for self-preservation. Givers navigate the delicate balance of compassion and discernment, choosing recipients judiciously to safeguard their well-being.

For those who have encountered the pain of being taken advantage of, it serves as a reminder that not every heart is prepared to receive the gift of generosity. However, this realization shouldn't close the door on the inherent goodness of giving. Instead, it extends an invitation to be selective, urging individuals to earn access to the precious gift of benevolence. A taker may resist releasing a giver, but the giver holds the power to decide who merits a place in their life. In the hustle of life's myriad experiences, where energies intersect, and intentions diverge, being a discerning giver emerges as a superpower—a gift that not only elevates the giver but also transforms the dynamics of relationships.

THE MONEY CODE:
CONVERSING WITH THE ADVISOR

Embarking on a journey to secure your financial future requires a strategic partnership with a reliable financial advisor. To ensure you're on the right path, it's crucial to ask pertinent questions and clearly communicate your investment preferences. Here are key points and inquiries to discuss with your financial advisor, guiding you toward informed choices and steady returns:

- **Market Approach:** Understand your advisor's market approach and investment strategy.
- **Company Preferences:** Request investments in top-performing companies across sectors, emphasizing simplicity and steady returns.
- **Specific Investments:** Express interest in renowned companies like Apple, Microsoft, Google, Nvidia, Eli Lily, and the SP 500 trust.
- **Market Downturn Strategy:** Communicate your strategy for capitalizing on market downturns, including purchasing preferred companies at discounted rates.
- **Equities and Bonds:** Inquire about the optimal balance between equities and bonds, seeking advice on diversification and potential

investment in US treasuries.

- **Risk Management:** Discuss risk management strategies, particularly in a declining market, to safeguard investments.
- **Real Estate Ventures:** Explore potential real estate ventures, such as flipping properties, utilizing Airbnb, or renting them out.
- **Regular Updates:** Express your desire for regular updates, requesting a comprehensive report every six months to stay well-informed about your financial portfolio.

Navigating the intricacies of financial decisions armed with insightful questions and clear expectations empowers you to make informed choices and cultivate a prosperous financial future. Your financial advisor is your ally in this pursuit, and effective communication is key to achieving your investment goals.

THE MONEY CODE: CONVERSING WITH THE ADVISOR (DECODED) - STREET SPEAK

Embarking on your grind to secure that bag? Linking up with a financial advisor who speaks your language is key. When you're chopping it up about your financial future, make sure you drop these questions and let your advisor know what's real. Here's the playbook:

- **Market Game:** Check how your advisor plays the market – what's their strategy?
- **Top-Notch Investments:** Tell your advisor you're looking for steady returns by investing in the big players across the board.
- **Big Players Only:** Ask for the hookup on companies like Apple, Microsoft, Google, Nvidia, Eli Lily, and the SP 500 trust.
- **Discount Moves:** Let them know you're ready to cop those top companies at a discount when the market takes a hit.
- **Mixing it Up:** Find out the play on balancing stocks and bonds, and if throwing down on US treasuries is a boss move.
- **No L's Here:** Discuss strategies to keep losses in check, especially when the market's on a downturn.
- **Real Estate Hustle:** Get the lowdown on real estate moves – flipping, Airbnb, or renting – what's the play?
- **Updates on Deck:** Tell your advisor you want the 411 regularly – a solid report every six months to keep your game tight.

When you're navigating the finance game, these questions are your street-smart playbook. Your advisor should be on the same grind as you, understanding your moves and speaking your language. Let's secure that bag together!

STREET-WISE: THE SMART GOALS EDITION

In the concrete jungle of chasing dreams, having a game plan is non-negotiable. Enter "Smart Goals" – more than a checklist, it's the blueprint to your success, a mindset that sets you on the path to bossing up. Imagine navigating the hustle with your goals as the roadmap, and Smart Goals as the street-smart sidekick breaking it down for you.

These aren't just any objectives. They're the ones that align with your grand vision, making every move count. Specific – no room for vague moves. Measurable – we're talking hard numbers, real talk. Achievable – conquering, not wishful thinking. Relevant – goals that matter in the grand scheme. Time-bound – no time to waste, on a mission. Whether in the urban jungle or chasing those grants, Smart Goals keep you focused, hustling, ticking off those objectives, and making every step count.

So, let's hustle smart, not just hard, turning dreams

into reality. With Smart Goals as your street-smart guide, each move is purposeful, each goal a step toward the future you're building. Time to boss up and hustle smart, paving the way for success in the concrete jungle of life.

RHYTHMS OF SUCCESS: THE FINANCIAL JOURNEY IN THE URBAN SYMPHONY

In the rhythmic dance of life, men aren't guided by a biological clock but by the pulse of a financial rhythm, echoing through the diverse city streets. Each man carves his own path, with some choosing the early steps of marriage and family, while others navigate different routes. Yet, the truth remains: societal judgments often center around a man's financial prowess, where money, though not the sole measure of manhood, plays a critical role.

The urban landscape doesn't shy away from casting judgments, acknowledging that money doesn't define a man's essence but recognizing the world's unkind perception when pockets aren't lined. Financial responsibility becomes a pivotal player, shaping individual destinies and family trajectories. Despite unexpected challenges arising from circumstances and past events, men are urged to align their ducks, grind hard, and strive for new heights in both life and career.

So, fellas, in this urban symphony, let's redefine what it means to have our "ish" together. It's not merely about money. It's about the hustle, the grind, and positioning ourselves for victories that truly matter. The judgments may linger in the city streets, but it's our moves that will resonate. Grind on, kings, and let's transform these concrete dreams into a vibrant reality.

EYES WIDE OPEN: THE RETINA HEIST

In the uncharted territory of success, there's a piece of street-smart wisdom that goes beyond the clichés – "Steal with your eyes." It's not about illicit actions but rather a call to sharpen your observational prowess. In a world where not everyone lays out the blueprint for success, this mantra encourages you to become a silent observer, absorbing the intricate details of those who have mastered their craft.

The key? Keep that mouth closed and let your eyes do the talking. Watch, learn, and internalize. The streets won't always serve lessons on a silver platter, but your ability to discern, adapt, and apply what you absorb is your secret weapon. It's a strategy that transcends the conventional narratives of success, urging you to be a silent force, absorbing the essence of expertise.

As you navigate this uncharted path, remember that silence is your ally. When you return, armed with the knowledge acquired through keen observation, you'll be ready to apply it in ways that defy expectations. This isn't about imitating. It's about internalizing, evolving, and then blowing people away with the unexpected depth of your insights.

THE
COMPANY YOU KEEP
REFLECTS
THE PATH YOU
WALK.

MASTERMIND EVOLUTION: FROM CRAFT TO KINGDOM

In the expansive realm of intellectual properties, the hustle doesn't end with mastering your craft. It evolves into a strategic game of thinking big and going global. The world is your canvas, and once you've honed your expertise, it's time to transcend the ordinary. This is not the moment for excuses. It's the juncture for redefining your results.

"Stand on business," you've invested time, sweat, and tears into becoming a maestro in your field. Now, it's about transforming that intellectual property into a multifaceted empire. It's about envisioning a legacy that extends beyond the confines of your immediate efforts. This is your cue to step into the realm of business coaching or consulting, where your insights become the cornerstone of others' success. The name of the game is residual income – ensuring that every ripple of your knowledge brings returns.

But here's the real talk – time is finite, and the grind can't be sustained indefinitely. It's time to chart new territories, to tap into avenues that offer both time and financial freedom. Imagine franchising your business, creating a network where your impact extends far beyond your personal capacity. Alternatively, envision starting a subscription service, where your business tips become a sought-after resource, and clients gladly pay a monthly fee for the invaluable insights you provide.

As you embark on this journey, remember, it's not just about what you've achieved. It's about the legacy you're building, the empire you're creating. The world is waiting for the next move in your intellectual chess game.

ACQUISITION CODE: THE CHESS OF IT ALL

When stepping into the realm of acquiring an existing business, it's no walk in the park – it's a dance, and you better lead. The first rule in this intricate tango is to question everything. No, not the casual small talk. We're talking interrogate with a purpose. People don't just sell businesses on a whim. There's a backstory, a motive lurking in the shadows. Some may try to cloak financial realities, luring you into a blindfolded purchase. Beware of the sweet talkers aiming to coax an offer out of you without revealing the financial skeletons in the closet.

As a savvy entrepreneur eyeing a potential acquisition, arm yourself with the right arsenal of questions. It's not just about the surface-level chit-chat.

Demand the nitty-gritty. Request their business schedule C, demand a peek at the K1 documents from the last two years, and insist on laying eyes on those W-2s. This isn't for show. It's your due diligence. Your detective work to unveil the true essence of what you're getting into.

Now, picture yourself at the negotiating table, and the current owner is trying to pull a fast one, playing hard to get with the financials. Hold your ground. It's a game, and the rules are clear. No financial transparency = no deal. It's not a matter of playing it safe. This is how you ensure and secure your future success. Don't be swayed by desperation or fancy sales pitches. A serious business owner looking to pass the torch will be an open book, transparent about the highs and lows of their brainchild.

So, potential business mogul, tread with caution, question with intention, and in the world of business acquisitions, ignorance is not bliss. It's a risky waltz. Master the moves, demand the details, and secure your empire. Let's call it the Acquisition Hustle—where every step is calculated, and every question is a key to the kingdom.

STRATEGIC LEVERAGE: YOUR LEASE, YOUR GAME

In the game of business, signing a lease is a strategic move that requires the finesse of a seasoned player. Before you put pen to paper, there's a crucial play you shouldn't skip: having a business attorney scrutinize that lease. It's not just about crossing your T's and dotting your I's. It's about making sure you're not stepping into a minefield of future headaches. Eager anticipation shouldn't blind you to the potential pitfalls lurking in the fine print. Your attorney becomes your strategic advisor, decoding the legal jargon and flagging any clauses that could turn your dream venture into a nightmare.

Don't be in a rush to seal the deal without understanding the game board. Your business deserves the best shot at longevity, and that starts with a lease that's not just a document but a roadmap to success. The CAM Fee, Tenant Reimbursement, rent-free months – these are moves you need to understand like the back of your hand. Your attorney is your coach, breaking down the plays and ensuring you're not left vulnerable to unforeseen damages or liabilities. It's about playing the game strategically, ensuring every move aligns with your long-term goals. So, before you take that step, consult your legal advisor.

DECODING WISDOM: ION FOOLIN' WITH THAT

"Ion foolin' with that." A timeless piece of wisdom echoing through the ages, passed down from the elders who knew a thing or two about navigating life's twists and turns. This ain't just a catchy phrase, it's a mantra for those who choose to keep it real and uncomplicated. So, let's break it down, street style.

In the tapestry of life, decisions can either be the stepping stones to success or the stumbling blocks to chaos. "Ion foolin' with that" is a commitment to authenticity. Our grandparents, the OGs of life's school, knew that a firm 'no' when needed is as powerful as a resounding 'yes' in the right direction. It's about listening to that gut feeling, that inner voice that speaks volumes when the world gets noisy.

Simplifying life – it's an art, a skill that comes with the wisdom of experience. "Ion foolin' with that" is an anchor in a sea of choices, a reminder that wavering in your decisions only leads to unnecessary complications. Whether it's relationships, opportunities, or the countless crossroads life throws at you, this saying is a compass guiding you to your truth.

So, when you hear those words, let them resonate – if you ain't foolin' with it, that's that. Embrace the power of decisiveness. Life is too short for maybes and uncertainties. Own your choices, and watch how simplicity becomes the ultimate sophistication in a world that often overcomplicates things.

TRUTH CODES:
THE POWER OF REPEATED WHYS

"**A**sk why 5 times" – a game-changing strategy straight from the school of life, where decoding truths is an art. In the complex dance of relationships, sometimes the real story lies beneath the surface, waiting to be unveiled. This ain't about being nosy, it's about understanding the why behind someone's actions, peeling back the layers for a deeper connection.

Picture this: you're navigating the intricate web of human interactions, and you come across a situation where transparency is key. That's when the magic of asking why 5 times kicks in. It's not just a matter of curiosity. It's a quest for authenticity. People often hold back, weaving a tapestry of half-truths and concealed motives. But by posing the why question repeatedly, you're not just seeking answers, you're unraveling the threads of their story, searching for consistency and patterns.

Now, let's get real about secrets. We've all got them, lurking in the shadows, fearing judgment or the prying eyes of others. But here's the truth: holding onto secrets is like carrying an unnecessary burden. The longer you wait, the heavier it becomes. "Ask why 5 times" is an invitation to lay it all out on the table, upfront and unfiltered. It's about giving others the chance to decide if they're in or out, based on the real, unvarnished truth.

So, in the grand symphony of human connections, don't be afraid to conduct the 'why' chorus. Peel away the layers, unravel the mysteries, and watch how authenticity becomes the melody that resonates in the hearts of those who choose to be real.

THE TWO-FACED IMPACT OF TRUTH: PAINFUL REVELATION, PRICELESS FREEDOM

In the raw reality of life, the truth stands as an unwavering force, and its impact is twofold – it hurts and remains unchanged. People often grapple with the discomfort that truth brings. Some attempt to sidestep it, to mold and twist it, or even drown it out with shouts and screams. But here's the real talk – any effort to manipulate the truth is just a veiled dance with deception. On the flip side, there are those bold souls who fearlessly embrace the truth, unafraid of its exposure. These individuals, who care little for the consequences, can be deemed dangerous in a world where vulnerability is often seen as weakness. Yet, in the timeless words of wisdom, the truth shall set you free.

Navigating the tapestry of human relationships, the truth becomes a beacon, piercing through the fog of falsehoods. Those who dare to confront it, head-on, find liberation. It's a powerful reckoning, a confrontation with reality that demands courage. The dichotomy lies in the choices we make when confronted with the truth – to crumble beneath its weight or to rise, emancipated, from the shackles of denial. In a world where honesty is both a rare commodity and a formidable weapon, understanding the transformative potential of the unadulterated truth is the key to breaking free from the chains that bind us.

So, in the grand theater of life, let's not shy away from the raw power of truth. Embrace it, even when it stings, for in its unaltered form lies the path to authentic freedom. This is the paradox of truth – simultaneously painful and liberating, an unyielding force that remains, undeterred, amidst the ever-shifting sands of life.

FROM SUITS TO SHOOTS: SHIELDING THE DREAM

Owning a business ain't just about the hustle and the grind. It's about securing what you've worked hard to build. Let's talk real. Every business owner, especially those running a cash cow, needs to have more than just their business acumen. It's about being street smart in the concrete jungle of entrepreneurship. Thieves ain't just eyeing your store, they're eyeing your success. They may not know the ins and outs of your business, but they know there's something worth taking. That's when you need to level up and get yourself a firearm.

In the game of business, you've got to be mindful 24/7. Watch your back walking into your business. Watch it leaving because there are eyes on you. Business robberies ain't spontaneous. They're calculated because they tend to watch their target's every move. So, stay in control and protect what's yours. Check the laws in your state and know your rights. If something feels off, trust your instincts. If someone's making your business their territory, ask them to step out. If they don't listen, don't hesitate to call the cops. And when it comes to protecting your life, draw that weapon if you gotta because in the urban hustle, it's not just about securing the bag, it's about securing your survival.

LIFE'S PLAYBOOK:
WHAT CODE DO YOU LIVE BY?

In the gritty reality of life, creating a criteria is like setting the rules of engagement for your own journey. Life is unpredictable, and you're bound to face challenges that can throw you off course. That's where your criteria comes in – it's the compass guiding you through the turbulent waters. Take a moment to list down what you want from life, your aspirations, and the standards you've set for yourself. This list isn't just a collection of dreams. It's a pact you make with yourself.

As you navigate the unpredictable twists and turns, your criteria becomes the benchmark against which you measure your actions. It's a call to accountability, a reminder not to veer too far from the path you've set for yourself. Life will throw distractions and temptations your way, but your criteria serves as a constant checkpoint, helping you stay focused and disciplined. It's about knowing your worth and refusing to settle for anything less. In the hustle of everyday life, having a criteria becomes your armor, protecting you from straying too far and ensuring that every step aligns with the life you've envisioned.

So, in the journey of life, lay down the rules that define your existence. Let your criteria be the silent force that whispers in your ear when things get tough. Stay disciplined, stay focused, and let your criteria be the unwavering foundation upon which you build the life you truly desire.

LOVE THYSELF: THE PRELUDE TO A HARMONIOUS CONNECTION

Embarking on the journey of self-discovery is a crucial step before diving into the complexities of dating. In the concrete jungle of relationships, it's essential to know yourself fully before attempting to understand someone else. Dating yourself is a powerful strategy for navigating the landscape of love. Take yourself out on dates, explore your interests, and let your soul soak in the experiences that truly resonate with you.

Picture this: a solo dinner at that fancy restaurant you've been eyeing, a spontaneous weekend getaway, or simply strolling through the city streets, reveling in the joy of your own company. These moments are a roadmap to self-awareness. When you're comfortable in your own skin, understanding your likes, dislikes, and aspirations, you become a more authentic and attractive partner. It's like laying the foundation for a skyscraper—sturdy, resilient, and ready to reach new heights.

Dating yourself is a dance with destiny. As you explore your own world, you might stumble upon someone who shares your vibe while you're out enjoying your own company. The universe works in mysterious ways, and sometimes, the right person comes into your life when you least expect it. So, in the symphony of self-love, play your own tune, dance to your rhythm, and let the magic of dating yourself set the stage for a harmonious connection with someone who resonates with your melody.

EMPIRE EXPANSION:
THE FRANCHISE FORTRESS

E xpanding your business empire is like playing chess in the game of entrepreneurship. Once your brand has garnered the respect and recognition it deserves, the idea of franchising becomes a strategic move to elevate your success. Don't let random individuals approach you with requests for a piece of your business without understanding the intricacies. Franchising provides a structured avenue to scale your business while allowing you to collect royalties for the hard-earned value you've built.

Imagine this as the grand strategy to fortify your business kingdom. Franchising not only opens doors for expansion but also acts as a shield against unnecessary inquiries. People might come with offers, but with franchising, you have a systematic way to filter those genuinely interested in the business model. It's like setting up a velvet rope – only those serious about investing and growing with your brand get access. This approach minimizes distractions and keeps the focus on what matters: strategic growth and sustained success.

So, as you navigate the terrain of entrepreneurship, consider franchising as your power move, a calculated step to extend the reach of your business legacy. Let the world see the blueprint of your success, and those genuinely interested will follow the path you've carefully paved.

BEYOND BARGAINS: THE ART OF CULTIVATING VALUABLE CLIENTS

In the world of entrepreneurship, the value of clients goes beyond their monetary contributions. The truth is, having the cheapest clients doesn't always equate to success. It can often lead to more headaches than benefits. When your prices are too low, it attracts a clientele that may not align with your business goals. These clients, driven primarily by the affordability factor, tend to bring a host of challenges—missed appointments, unreasonable behavior, and an overall strain on your time and resources.

Starting out might require some flexibility, doing what you must to build a foundation. However, as you climb the ladder of success, it becomes imperative to seek clients who understand the value of your time and expertise. Elevating your business means attracting clients who are willing to elevate with you, those who respect and appreciate the quality of your craft. It's not just about the transaction but building relationships with clients who see the worth in what you bring to the table.

In the entrepreneurial journey, the goal is not just to accumulate clients but to cultivate a client base that aligns with your vision. The cheapest clients may seem like a quick fix, but in the long run, investing in clients who understand and value your worth is the key to sustained success.

CASH MOVES: WHEN BANKS CLOSE, BE YOUR OWN BACK-UP PLAN

In the hustle of entrepreneurship, navigating the financial landscape can be a game-changer. When the traditional route of securing a loan hits a dead-end, it's time to play a different hand – become your own bank. The old saying holds true: cash is king. It holds a power that credit can't quite match. Dodging the complexities and potential rejections from banks, consider running your own funds up. Living below your means and investing your own cash into your business minimizes the red tape, making it a straightforward and less cumbersome process.

By fronting your own business, you're essentially placing a bet on yourself. It's a bold move that eliminates the need to owe anybody, and whatever returns come your way are yours to claim. The beauty of this approach lies in the simplicity and self-reliance it affords. Living by the mantra of "cash is king," you're not dependent on external approvals. If one avenue closes, you pivot, relying on your resourcefulness and resilience. Betting on yourself becomes a mantra, and as you do it once, the confidence to do it again becomes second nature. When banks close their doors, you become the backup plan – a strategy that's rooted in self-reliance and entrepreneurship.

LONGEVITY CODE

In the realm of professional longevity, mastering the art of customer relations and continuous self-improvement holds the key to a thriving career. From attentive listening to staying well-equipped, the journey towards sustained success involves a strategic blend of skills, adaptability, and a commitment to ongoing education. Let's delve into the core principles that unlock the doors to enduring excellence.

- **Be a Good Listener:** Foster meaningful connections with customers and colleagues by paying attention to distinctive details. Remembering names, inquiring about their lives, hobbies, or work creates a foundation for engaging conversations on subsequent encounters.

- **Accommodating:** Prioritize meeting the needs of both customers and coworkers. A flexible and accommodating approach fosters positive relationships, contributing to a harmonious work environment.

- **Continued Education:** Choose a specialized school for ongoing education, ensuring your skills stay relevant in a dynamic professional landscape. Completing courses, obtaining certificates, and pursuing additional master classes are crucial steps in evolving and staying ahead in your field.

- **Equipment (Always Have Enough Tools in the Toolbox):** Invest in brand new supplies before entering the workforce. A well-equipped toolbox not only enhances your enthusiasm for the job but also allows you to experiment with new tools, refining your craft. Knowing the right tools for specific tasks is instrumental in ensuring the quality of your work.

As we navigate the intricacies of professional longevity, these keys become the guiding principles that open doors to sustained success. The commitment to customer engagement, adaptability, continuous learning, and well-equipped craftsmanship forms a powerful combination for a lasting and fulfilling career journey.

LEADING IN THE SHADOWS: NAVIGATING THE UNKNOWNS OF EMPLOYEE WELL-BEING

In the world of business ownership and leadership, being the last to know can often be an unavoidable reality. As a leader, the responsibility to steer the ship is paramount, but the challenge lies in the personal matters of employees that might go unnoticed. It's not uncommon for those in leadership positions to find themselves out of the loop when it comes to the personal struggles their team members are facing – legal troubles, relationship woes, substance abuse, child support issues, or family conflicts. Employees tend to share these aspects with each other while keeping their leaders in the dark. The dynamic is such that they may not disclose what's really going on despite their supervisors observing subtle changes in behavior.

This lack of insight can pose a threat to effective leadership, with potential consequences that are beyond the leader's control. Employees might keep personal challenges hidden until it becomes a pressing issue, forcing the leader into damage control mode. As an owner or manager, it becomes imperative to anticipate that employees might not be forthright about their personal struggles. To bridge this gap, implementing regular wellness checks or questionnaires every three months can provide a snapshot of the team's mental well-being. The goal is to prevent situations where an employee is mentally checked out but still going through the motions at work, as this can inevitably impact their performance, subsequently affecting the overall health of the business.

In the intricate dance of leadership, staying attuned to the heartbeat of your team's well-being is a delicate yet essential choreography. By acknowledging the challenges of being the last to know, leaders can proactively address the potential pitfalls and foster a workplace culture where open communication about personal challenges is not just encouraged but prioritized.

STEALTH MOVES: CRAFTING YOUR PATH IN PURPOSEFUL SILENCE

Navigating life without a clear direction is akin to spinning your wheels in a world full of movement and momentum. It's the equivalent of being the loudest dog in the neighborhood, drawing attention without substantial strength. We've all seen that dog, barking tirelessly, making noise, yet lacking true impact. The real power lies in the stealthy, unpredictable ones, the dogs you don't see coming. In the hustle of life, it's crucial to emulate the latter – be the unexpected force, quietly making strides and catching everyone off guard.

The essence of the message is simple: craft a plan and set it in motion. Life demands direction, purpose, and deliberate action. Too often, individuals get caught in the trap of making loud announcements without the corresponding substance of accomplishment. It's a reminder to operate with more action and fewer declarations. Life favors those who move strategically, executing plans with precision rather than those who simply make noise without tangible progress.

In a world full of distractions and clamor, the real movers and shakers are the ones who don't broadcast every move but make significant strides in silence. So, make your plan, commit to the journey, and let your actions speak louder than any proclamation.

BEYOND THE THRONE: STAYING RICH BY ELEVATING YOUR TEAM

As a boss in the game, climbing the ladder to success extends beyond stacking up your own chips. It's about lifting your whole crew with you. The key to staying rich isn't hoarding wealth but empowering your circle. Picture it like a strategic chess move. You're not only making decisions for the present, you're grooming the next player to take the lead. When your company hits a point where it needs a lieutenant, it's time to look within, find the talent, and elevate someone to that pivotal role.

Empowering from within a trust builder. Your team needs to see that you're not only about personal gains but creating opportunities for them too. When you promote someone from the ranks, it sends a clear message – goals are attainable, and hard work doesn't go unnoticed. Having a lieutenant enables you to delegate tasks as well as instill leadership qualities. That new captain sees the game through your lens, learning from your triumphs and, yes, your mistakes. As a boss, you're building a legacy, one empowered lieutenant at a time.

So, bosses, it's time to hire that lieutenant, not just as a backup but as a strategic move to strengthen your empire. When you've got good foot soldiers following a capable leader, that's how you play the long game and secure lasting success.

BIN BASICS: STREAMLINING BUSINESS CLEANLINESS

Navigating the terrain of running a business involves paying attention to even the smallest details, like the unsung heroes – trash cans. Imagine setting up your shop, ready to make strides in the world of success. Now, let's keep it real – don't go overboard with the trash cans. It might seem like a good idea to load up, thinking you're covered, but too many only lead to chaos. Staff and customers alike will fill them up, creating unnecessary work for you. And those massive bins? Just an invitation for overflows and added headaches.

Finding that sweet spot is the key – just enough trash cans at the right size. Keep things manageable. But the game doesn't end there. Your team needs to be on top of it. Daily wipe-downs and routine trash duties are a must. Let's face it, nobody wants the stench of yesterday's lunch lingering around. It's not just about cleanliness, it's about creating an environment where customers want to stay. And if things get a bit funky, keep a can of Febreze handy. Because in the fast-paced world of business, every detail counts, even the trash cans.

VIBIN' AND THRIVIN'

Navigating the business landscape of 2024 demands a shift in mindset. These days it's all about the vibes and the thrive. As customers step into your establishment, it's not merely about products or services, it's a holistic experience. Imagine a space where the beats create a rhythm, aesthetics paint an inviting atmosphere, and the overall ambiance becomes an irresistible draw. Your business transforms into a curated destination for catching the right vibes.

To truly thrive, you must embrace the role of a vibe curator. The music becomes the heartbeat, the visual aesthetics set the mood, and your online presence extends the encounter beyond physical boundaries. It's about creating an atmosphere that beckons, making customers feel compelled to be part of it. With features like step and repeat walls, your business becomes a social media sensation, a highlight in their day that they can't help but share. In this new era, thriving is no longer about transactions but about sculpting an environment where customers immerse themselves in the vibes, creating a desire to return for the unforgettable experience.

APPROVAL SAGA: THE PATH TO OPENING DAY

When you open up a business, it's not just a snap of a finger. There are so many things that go into it. One of the most crucial aspects is obtaining your construction permit. The approval process can take weeks or even months, potentially delaying your business's opening. Once you've signed your lease, the countdown begins, but certain factors are beyond your control. The pace of progress is dictated by the approval timeline of the county you're in. Here are the steps involved in securing your construction permit:

- **Apply for a permit:** Schedule an appointment or go online to your local city hall to initiate the permit application process for your business.
- **Pay permit fees:** Once the application is submitted, the applicant must pay the initial fee assessment before the plan review can commence.
- **Plan and Review:** City staff reviews all construction permit applications for compliance with building codes, environmental regulations, zoning codes, and other applicable rules.

- **Permit Card Insurance:** After approval, the city stamps the construction drawings and issues a Permit Card, indicating compliance.
- **Inspections:** Inspections at project milestones ensure adherence to state-adopted building codes; failure to follow inspection codes risks fines and shutdowns.
- **Plan Modifications:** Submit revisions to your drawings through plan modifications after the Permit Card has been issued, subject to the same review process.
- **As-Built Drawings:** Staff uses these to confirm that the project aligns with the approved construction documents.
- **Certificate of Completion/Occupancy:** Required for all new additions and alterations, confirming compliance and allowing occupancy, especially for residences occupied during construction.

Navigating the permit process is a critical dance, and understanding these steps can help you choreograph your business opening smoothly. It's the key to unlocking the doors of your establishment. Don't rush the process. Work with it, ensuring that each step is well-executed for a successful grand opening.

DELEGATE

THEN

ELEVATE

LOVE & LEGACY: ELEVATING RELATIONSHIPS BEYOND LUST

I n the sphere of relationships, it's time for men to level up and redefine the narrative. Bragging about conquests might be the talk of the town, but there's a higher game to play. It's not about how many you've been with, it's about the richness you've gained by choosing a partner wisely. It's about finding a woman worth the investment, someone who resonates beyond the physical.

Before diving into the sea of relationships, it's essential to discern where a woman's priorities lie. It's not about perfection but about worthiness. Beyond the fleeting pleasures, it's about building something meaningful together. In a world where recreational connections are rampant, a man with vision seeks a  woman with discipline. The goal is to elevate each other, create a legacy, and put a ring on a finger that signifies partnership in both love and business.

For the kings out there, it's time to save yourself

from the heartbreak and drama that comes with frivolous connections. Listen to your spirit, seek meaningful companionship, and invest your time where it matters. Find someone who adds value to your life, someone worth every moment of your precious time. Wake up, kings – the journey to fulfillment begins with choosing someone who aligns with your vision.

LIMITLESS DREAMS: SURROUNDING YOURSELF WITH VICTORY

In the landscape of life, encountering self-limiting individuals can be a common hurdle. These are the folks who find comfort in the familiar, resistant to the allure of new experiences, opportunities, or relationships that beckon beyond their comfort zones. While it's acceptable to coexist with them, it's crucial not to let their self-limiting energy cast shadows on your aspirations. Whether it's embarking on new adventures, starting a business, or pursuing your dreams, don't let their reluctance hold you back. Recognize that their journey is different, and your path may lead to places they can't envision.

Surrounding yourself with people who uplift and motivate becomes imperative in this scenario. Seek companions who resonate with your dreams, individuals who inspire you to strive for victories. The battle is inherently you versus yourself, and succumbing to the influence of self-limiting individuals can shackle your potential. Embrace those who encourage you to believe in the impossible, understanding that your goals are achievable despite any external doubts. In the end, your success is determined by your determination to overcome self-imposed limitations.

ROAD WARRIORS: CHARTING SUCCESS IN A BEAT-AROUND

Embarking on the road to success is a journey that demands a considerable amount of time behind the wheel. In this hustle, your choice of a car becomes more about practicality than flaunting flashy status symbols. Opting for a beat-around car, perhaps an older Honda, Acura, or Corolla, becomes the smart move. These vehicles serve the purpose of getting you from point A to point B without draining your pockets. The essence lies in functionality, not luxury. As you step out of your ride, it's all about the grind – time to hustle, time to make moves.

A low-maintenance car becomes your companion on this entrepreneurial journey, a vehicle that doesn't demand an excessive investment. It's about wisely choosing a car that won't break the bank, considering the realities of the road – accidental dents, rocks hitting your window, unexpected traffic, bad weather, and unforeseen accidents. Your focus should be on the hustle, not on the glamor of your ride. Save the shining moments for later. Calculate your daily mileage, align it with your needs, and make a practical choice. As you navigate the challenges of the road, remember, the real shine comes from the victories you achieve along the way.

ROOM CONVERSATIONS: BEYOND CITY DREAMS

Picture this: we're sitting in a room, having a real talk about making moves and seeking a fresh start. You know, a lot of folks think packing up and heading to a city like Atlanta or Houston is the magic fix for all their problems. It's like this golden ticket to a brand-new life. But, let me tell you something real – changes don't just happen because you changed your address. It all starts from within, not by switching cities. And hey, no shade to Atlanta or Houston, but they're not the cure-all for your personal stuff.

Now, I get it. The allure of a new city, the promise of better weather, more opportunities, and attractive people – it's tempting. But here's the truth: moving to a new place doesn't automatically wipe the slate clean. Your problems don't just vanish. People might come to Atlanta thinking they can reinvent themselves, and that's cool, but you've got to do the work on yourself first. All those opportunities will still be waiting, but the real game-changer is what you do internally.

Let's keep it a buck about the size of these cities. Atlanta, for example, ain't as massive as it might seem. It's like a small town with a big reputation. So, how you carry yourself matters. Your behavior can echo across the city – affecting your business, your friendships, and your love life. It's all connected.

And here's a little humor for you – thinking you can escape your issues by moving, but guess what? If you can't make it here, you might just find yourself back where you started or trying your luck in Houston. Life's funny like that.

So, as we chop it up in this room, remember this: true transformation starts with you, not with a change of scenery. It's about doing the inner work before you start a new chapter. Success in a city of opportunities is about growing personally. Keep it authentic, stay grounded, and watch how you'll navigate the real changes.

VISUALIZING VICTORY: THE ART OF LIFE'S CHOICES

Let's break it down – you're sitting there, thinking about making moves, and the big question hits you: What does that look like? It's the kind of question that can either guide you to success or make you rethink everything. Most folks have this picture-perfect idea in their heads of what they want. They're like, "Yeah, I want that life." But hold up – reality and perception don't always shake hands.

Here's the real deal – nothing worth having comes easy. What you think you want might hit you with a reality check once you realize the hustle it demands. It's like, "Is this what I signed up for?" You gotta ask yourself, what does it really look like if I dive into this? And, equally important, what does it look like if I don't?

People often jump into things without figuring out their why – the driving force behind their decisions. It's a crucial step, my friend. Your choices shape your short-term grind and the long trajectory of your life. Visualize: where do you want to be in a few years? What's your life vibe? Who and what do you want in it? You're essentially curating your story, and every decision adds a chapter. So, ask yourself, do the moves I'm making now age well?

In the grand scheme of things, it's about making decisions that align with the vision you have for your life. It's about understanding the look of your journey, both the challenges and the victories. After all, the choices you make today will paint the picture of your tomorrow.

CASH FIRST, LOVE SECOND: THE POWER OF DEPOSITS

Let's keep it real – running a business ain't a walk in the park, especially when you're juggling a hectic schedule. As professionals, we love our clients, but we also love our money. That's why you gotta play smart and charge a deposit. Life throws curveballs, and you can't afford to miss out on that hard-earned cash due to unforeseen circumstances.

Make it easy, keep it simple, and slap a nonrefundable deposit on the table. When clients book, let them know they gotta have that credit card on file. Protect your revenue and the essence of your hustle. And hey, to my fellow business owners dealing with unlicensed entrepreneurs in the mix, take that $500 deposit. State boards could be lurking around any corner, and you sure as heck don't want fines raining down or risking that precious license.

Think of it as an insurance policy for your business. Cover your back, cover your hustle. No business can afford to take a hit, and you shouldn't be left scrambling. So, don't play with fire. Protect your business at all costs.

NO GAMES, NO GIMMICKS: SETTING THE RECORD STRAIGHT ON SERVICES

Imagine this scenario: you're hustling hard, running your business, and clients try to pull a fast one on you. Yeah, we've all been there. Some folks book the budget service but have their eyes on the deluxe treatment, thinking they can slide under the radar. It's a classic move – trying to get over and snag a pricier service without shelling out the extra dough. But hold up, we ain't falling for that.

Let's keep it real – your services are priced for a reason, and clients need to play by the rules. If they book a specific service on your site, that's what they should be getting. Anything extra comes with an upcharge – no freebies here. In this game, honesty is the name of the game, but not everyone's playing fair. Not every client is your ideal client, and some will go to great lengths to save a few bucks on services they don't want to pay for. Don't let that chaos slide into your business. Stand your ground on those prices, and if they can't afford it, kindly show them the exit. There's no room for back-and-forth games – find clients who respect your hustle and the value you bring.

So, here's the golden rule: don't let clients call your services something different from what it is. Hold the line, stand tall, and attract those clients who not only appreciate but respect your business. It's a two-way street, and you're worth every penny.

INVENTORY:
LOCK IT UP TIGHT & THROW AWAY THE KEY

In business, you learn real quick that trust is like gold, and you can't afford to lose it. Understand that not everyone strolling through your doors has your back. Some are scheming for a quick come-up that could straight-up mess with your hustle. Your inventory? That's your lifeblood, and protecting it ain't up for debate.

Your objective is to lock it up tight and throw away the key. Only the chosen few should hold the code: you and your trusted manager. Not all employees are loyal soldiers. Some are wolves in sheep's clothing, ready to snatch what they can as soon as you turn your back. Cameras become your silent guardians, witnessing every move, every motive.

A theft, a hit to your inventory, could send shockwaves through your business. It's not just about losing goods, it's about losing time, shutting down, losing staff, and the domino effect that follows. Prevention is your armor, surveillance cameras are your eyes, and a locked inventory is your shield. Give the code only to those who've earned it, and change it like your business depends on it because it does.

In this harsh reality, some folks are out for themselves, blind to the impact on others. Thieves don't care about the sweat, sacrifice, and dreams that built your business. They're after a quick score. So, in the concrete jungle, govern yourself and your business wisely. Protect your livelihood, because it's not just about surviving, it's about thriving against all odds.

CLIENT CODE:
GIVE 'EM WHAT THEY WANT

In the hustle of running a business, there's one golden rule—give the people what they want, no questions asked. It's the secret sauce to longevity. Now, let's keep it real. Being an entrepreneur ain't about imposing your preferences on clients. It's about delivering exactly what they crave. Whether it's a haircut, a meal, or a service, the customer is the VIP, and they want to walk out feeling on top of the world. Keep it simple, keep it consistent – that's the key. Switch up on them, and trust, they'll switch up on you real quick. It's like this unspoken contract – you provide what they desire, and they'll keep coming back for more.

Sure, you can drop suggestions, maybe even throw in a collaborative vibe, but at the end of the day, it's all about putting the client first. Their experience with you, that's your business card. Be the one who always delivers, who never disappoints, because in this game, customers aren't just buying a product or service, they're investing in an experience. So, if you want to ride the wave of success, remember this mantra: give the people what they want, every single time. They're not just judging your business, they're judging you by the experience you provide.

HUSTLER'S DIARY: TRACKING THE DOLLARS AND SENSE

L et's cut to the chase for all you hustlers out there. Tracking numbers ain't a luxury, it's a survival skill in the game of business. No room for excuses. So, here's the drill: arm yourself with a trusty notebook and a slick calendar. That notebook? It's your hustle log—every client, every dollar, every day. Now, the calendar. It's not just about dates, it's your financial diary. Daily, jot down what's rolling in, and double down by writing it in the notebook too.

Now, here's the game-changer – when January 1st hits, grab a fresh calendar, a clean slate for your financial journey. End of each month, no slacking, tally it up, face the cold, hard facts. Because if you're running a business and you don't know the monthly digits, you're playing a risky game. A true entrepreneur? They write it all down, keeping that daily guide close. It's about the sense to know your numbers, inside and out.

And let's not forget the power of reflection. Take a moment each month to analyze those numbers, learn from them, and strategize for the road ahead. It's not just about tracking, it's about evolving, adapting, and staying ahead in the financial game.

FROM STRUGGLES TO TRIUMPHS: UNCOVERING THE GLORY IN YOUR STORIES

Let me drop some wisdom for all you hustlers out there. The real power, the true magic of entrepreneurship, lies in your stories. It ain't just about the products or services you're selling, it's about the connection, the vibe, the personal touch. As an entrepreneur, you're more than a seller. You're a storyteller, and that, my friend, is the secret sauce.

See, people come to your business for more than the goods, they come for you. If you can spin a good yarn, share bits of your journey, and lay it out there. You're selling an experience. Open up, be real, let them peek behind the curtain. People love authenticity–it's magnetic. When they see the person behind the business, it humanizes the whole experience. It makes them comfortable, like they're dealing with a friend. And let's be honest, we're all navigating through this crazy journey called life. Your struggles, victories, and lessons resonate. It's a reminder that we're not alone in the struggle, we're all fighting similar battles.

Now, here's the kicker. It's not just about growing your business, it's about growing yourself. When you open up, when you share your stories, you're not just giving to your customers, you're receiving too. It's therapeutic, a two-way street of connection. Your mental health gets a boost, and you might just find clarity in your own experiences. Plus, you become that go-to person, that listening ear, that beacon of advice. People appreciate that, and they can't wait to come back, not just for your products but for the shared stories. So, hustle hard, but remember, the glory truly is in your stories.

BLUEPRINTS AND BUDGETS: CRAFTING YOUR BUSINESS SPACE WISELY

Embarking on the journey of starting a business is a thrilling adventure, but one that demands careful financial navigation. Your budget becomes the compass guiding your decisions, and a crucial aspect is the architectural design and general contractor quote. Picture this as the blueprint of your dreams taking shape – the foundation that sets the tone for your entire venture. To get this right, wisdom lies in gathering at least three quotes from distinct general contractors and architects. It's not about choosing the highest or the lowest but finding that sweet spot where quality meets affordability.

In this game, referrals are your golden ticket. Ask around, seek recommendations, and delve into their portfolios. You want someone licensed, bonded, and insured – a qualified maestro turning your vision into reality. Your project is a significant investment, and you deserve top-notch service. Don't shy away from asking the tough questions. After all, surprises aren't welcome in the business world. This is your turf, and you want your architect and general contractor to deliver excellence. As you gather those three separate quotes, it's about more than numbers – it's about weighing the pros and cons, finding the perfect fit that aligns with your vision and budget.

So, hustle wisely, compare diligently, and when the time comes to make that decision, you'll have a blueprint not just for your space but for your success. Because in the realm of business, the right foundation sets the stage for greatness.

SOULFUL CONNECTIONS: A JOURNEY CLOSER TO GOD

In the journey of life, the essence of relationships goes beyond the surface, reaching deeper into the spiritual realm. Wisdom shines through the mantra, "Closer to God," which echoes a fundamental truth that our connections should be conduits for spiritual elevation. It's a declaration that resonates with the soul, urging us to evaluate the relationships that shape our existence. In the tapestry of human connections, the thread that intertwines with our journey toward God is the one worth weaving into our lives.

Scripture teaches us the significance of surrounding ourselves with those who uplift our spirit and draw us nearer to God. As Proverbs 13:20 wisely states, "Walk with the wise and become wise, for a companion of fools suffers harm." The quality of our relationships is a reflection of the spiritual path we tread. If we find ourselves regressing instead of progressing, it's time to reevaluate the company we keep.

Consider the powerful testimony of Psalm 1:1-3, illustrating the impact of our associations on our spiritual growth: "Blessed is the one who does not walk in step with the wicked or stand in the way that sinners take or sit in the company of mockers, but whose delight is in the law of the Lord, and who meditates on his law day and night. That person is like a tree planted by streams of water, which yields its fruit in season and whose leaf does not wither—whatever they do prospers." This serves as a poignant reminder that our connections should be sources of spiritual nourishment, propelling us to flourish in our journey toward God.

So, in a nutshell, the statement "Closer to God" encapsulates a timeless truth—the relationships we foster should be instruments of spiritual ascension. They should contribute to our growth as individuals, drawing us closer to God with each step. It's a testament to the transformative power of intentional connections that shape not just our earthly existence but our eternal journey.

Milton Keynes UK
Ingram Content Group UK Ltd.
UKHW020245300424
441938UK00002B/18